John Milton

Paradise Lost Book 1

Introduction by Catherine Thom son

Explanatory Notes by Anna Baldwir

OCR
RECOGNISING ACHIEVEMENT

O
U

Official Publisher

D0416373

OXFORD
UNIVERSITY PRESS

Great Clarendon Street, Oxford OX2 6DP

Oxford University Press is a department of the University of Oxford.
It furthers the University's objective of excellence in research, scholarship,
and education by publishing worldwide in

Oxford   New York

Auckland   Cape Town   Dar es Salaam   Hong Kong   Karachi
Kuala Lumpur   Madrid   Melbourne   Mexico City   Nairobi
New Delhi   Shanghai   Taipei   Toronto

With offices in

Argentina   Austria   Brazil   Chile   Czech Republic   France   Greece
Guatemala   Hungary   Italy   Japan   South Korea   Poland   Portugal
Singapore   Switzerland   Thailand   Turkey   Ukraine   Vietnam

Oxford is a registered trade mark of Oxford University Press
in the UK and in certain other countries

British Library Cataloguing in Publication Data
Data available

ISBN: 978-019-838688 9
10 9 8 7 6 5 4 3 2 1

Typeset in India by TNQ

Printed in Great Britain by CPI Antony Rowe, Chippenham

Paper used in the production of this book is a natural, recyclable product made
from wood grown in sustainable forests. The manufacturing process conforms
to the environmental regulations of the country of origin.

Contents

Introduction: English Literature

Unit F663 is the examined unit for English Literature A2, and carries 60% of the marks at A2. This text has been prescribed for Section B of the examination, where you are required to explore connections and comparisons between a drama text and a poetry text. In this introduction, you will find advice to help you prepare for the examination and the ways in which your work will be assessed.

Choice of texts

For Section B study, there is a choice of four drama texts and four poetry texts; your teacher will select one text from each group of four. There is a free choice of pairings of texts, and your teacher will look for connections between the texts he or she chooses. For example, there may be similarities of tone (e.g. humorous or heroic) or of subject matter (e.g. religious faith or the treatment of women). When you are preparing for the examination, it will be important to ensure that you know the individual texts in detail, and also that you have considered very thoroughly the possible connections and comparisons between them.

How to approach the examination

There will be a choice of six questions of which you can choose any one, regardless of your choice of set texts. These questions will ask about a central idea (e.g. power, or tragedy, or the role of women), and ask you to compare the treatment of this idea in your chosen texts.

For example, an essay question might read:

> By comparing one poetry and one drama text you have studied, discuss ways in which writers explore the dangers and delights of ambition.

The question begins by asking for comparison. You should understand this as an invitation to look for any similarities or differences, or any other connections between the two texts which help you to answer the question (see AO3 below). Most questions will ask you to look at 'ways in which' the writer treats the area under discussion; this part of the question directs you to consider the variety of approaches and methods used by writers in their treatment of the central theme or idea (see AO2 below). It is important to look carefully at the way the question is worded: in the question currently under discussion, for example, you are not just invited to discuss the theme of 'ambition' – you are asked to consider 'the <u>dangers and delights</u> of ambition'. To receive high marks, therefore, you need to consider carefully and explicitly both the destabilising and the rewarding qualities of ambition in your answer.

In an English Literature examination, there is never just one correct way to answer the question; however, there are some useful techniques which may help you to maximise your marks. It is helpful to write a short introduction to your essay which addresses the central idea in the question and relates it briefly to the texts you have chosen. The main body of your essay should include detailed discussion of the central idea, relating it to both of your set texts. You should ensure that you give the two texts roughly equal space in your answer, and that you include passages of sustained comparison: answers which deal with the two texts separately – perhaps with some perfunctory comparison by way of conclusion – will limit the marks they can achieve for looking at 'connections and comparisons' (see AO3 below). Finally, you should consider writing a conclusion which expresses succinctly the most important similarities and/or differences between your two texts in relation to the central idea in the question.

You should aim to use quotations to support your answer, especially with reference to AO2 (see below). Remember that AO2 can also be satisfied by more general references to the text, however, so that your own brief account of an event or moment in the text will sometimes be as helpful as a quotation.

What are the Assessment Objectives?

Your examiner will mark your work on the basis of four

Assessment Objectives (AO1, AO2, AO3 and AO4); the marking will be weighted in favour of AO3 and AO4.

Assessment Objective 1

> Articulate **creative, informed** and **relevant** responses to literary texts, using **appropriate terminology and concepts**, and **coherent, accurate written expression**.

Answers should be **creative** in the sense that good candidates will respond imaginatively, selecting and combining interesting and telling moments from the poetry and drama texts which help to arrive at an answer to the question.

They should be **informed** by a reasonable level of awareness concerning the set texts; for example, of information about the writers, the nature of poems or plays of the period in question and of poetry and drama in general. Such information should support the answer but not be allowed to dominate it.

Above all, answers should be **relevant**: when writing practice essays, it can be helpful to check every sentence to ensure that it is helping to form an answer to the question. You should aim to use key terms from the question at times during your essay, and especially in the conclusion.

During your study of your set texts, you should become familiar with **appropriate terminology and concepts**: for example, you should be able to discuss ideas such as 'dramatic irony' and 'metaphor'.

Coherent, accurate written expression is an essential part of a good answer: you should check the accuracy of your spelling and punctuation and especially your grammar to ensure that your essay is completed to a high standard and can be readily understood.

Assessment Objective 2

> Demonstrate **detailed critical understanding** in **analysing** the ways in which **structure, form and language** shape meanings in literary texts.

This Assessment Objective requires you to look closely at the detail of your set texts. You need to show how the writer of your poem or play achieves his or her effects through choices of language, form and structure. Methods of writing will vary according to the text you are studying: comments on **language** might include references to allusion (e.g. Pope's use of classical reference in *The Rape of the Lock*) or dialogue (e.g. polite conversation in *The School for Scandal*). Writing about **form** might lead you to consider choices the writer has made within his or her chosen genre (aspects of the revenge tragedy in *The Duchess of Malfi*, for example, or the use of the sonnet form in John Donne). Material relating to **structure** might focus on a writer's use of contrasting passages (e.g. scenes in *Dr Faustus* dealing with Faustus's enjoyments and those with his damnation, or Milton's use of narrative and dialogue in *Paradise Lost*). Remember, it is not enough to list methods used by a writer, even if you offer examples; you must always analyse the effects of the writing as well.

Assessment Objective 3

> **Explore connections and comparisons between different literary texts**, informed by interpretations of other readers.

This Assessment Objective combines different ideas, and here the main requirement is that you should **explore connections and comparisons** between your poetry and drama texts. During your answer, you should ensure that you offer some detailed and sustained comparison to show how the poet and the playwright you have studied compare in their treatment of the theme or idea in the question. You might find differences or similarities in the attitudes revealed in the text, or in the techniques used to express ideas (if you compare techniques, you will find that you are responding to AO2 and AO3 at the same time). You will find it helpful to bear in mind important features of the genre in which each text has been written. You can also receive credit for evidence that your answer is informed by **interpretations of other readers**, but this aspect of AO3 is of secondary importance in this section of the paper.

Assessment Objective 4

> Demonstrate understanding of the significance and influence of the **contexts** in which literary texts are written and received.

This Assessment Objective requires you to think about ideas and information in addition to the set texts. These ideas might be social or historical (e.g. what was the role of women in society at the time your text is written or is set?); they could be literary (what is this text like in relation to others by the same writer, or by his or her contemporaries?); they could be biographical (what were the important influences on the life of the writer when he or she produced this work?). It is also helpful to consider different critical reactions to the text over the period of time since its publication – or, in the case of drama, the performance history of your chosen play. In this part of the exam, it will be especially helpful to consider your set texts in the context of the genre in which they were written (see 'Cross-genre Comparison' below). Contextual study requires some research and learning, but should never be allowed to dominate an answer; take care to avoid writing long paragraphs of contextual information which do not support your argument.

Cross-genre Comparison

One of the most demanding aspects of this section is the requirement for 'cross-genre comparison'. At AS level, you will have covered techniques for comparison of two texts in Task 2 of your coursework unit; however, these texts may well have been from the same genre, so that you were comparing like with like. In Section B of F663, as in your A2 coursework, you are required to compare texts from different genres: here, poetry and drama, and, in your coursework, poetry and prose. For this reason, you will find it especially helpful to investigate and discuss characteristics of the genres of your chosen texts, and to use this study as part of the basis for your comparison. You might wish to ask yourself some of the following questions about the texts you are studying:

- What are the chief characteristics of drama? (Think about characters, action, dialogue, conflict, the role of the audience, etc.)
- What are the chief characteristics of poetry? (Think about form, imagery, concentration of linguistic effect, etc.)
- How 'poetic' is my drama text? (Is it written completely or partly in verse? Does the writer make significant use of poetic techniques such as elaborate similes or couplets?)
- How 'dramatic' is my poetry text? (Does it have a narrative line? Characters? A strong speaking voice? Does it include passages which deal with action or conflict? Does it lend itself to performance?)
- Why might a poet and a dramatist treat an idea or a theme in a different way? What are the constraints and opportunities offered by these different genres?

If you can supply detailed answers to these questions, preferably with textual support (detailed references or quotations), you will have completed some very effective preparation for this part of the exam. You may also like to use an appropriately adapted version of these questions to support your A2 coursework preparation; it certainly makes sense to be aware of the similarities of these two tasks, so that you can transfer the skills you learn between them.

OCR Specification Excerpt

The OCR GCE specification for English Literature is the document on which assessment is based; it specifies the content and skills to be covered in delivering a course of study. At all times, therefore, these excerpts should be read in conjunction with the specification. If clarification on a particular point is needed then reference should be in the first instance to the specification.

Unit Content

A2 Unit F663: *Drama and Poetry pre-1800* (Closed text)

There are two sections to this unit:

• Section A: Shakespeare
• *Section B: Drama and Poetry pre-1800*

Section B: Drama and Poetry pre-1800

This section requires candidates to explore contrasts, connections and comparisons between different literary texts. In their answers candidates must refer to **one drama text** and **one poetry text** from the lists of texts set for this section.

There will be a choice of six different questions each with a different focus. Candidates must select **one** question, and base their answer on a comparative study, with substantial discussion of both texts.

Candidates are required to show critical understanding in analysing ways in which structure, form and language shape meaning and demonstrate understanding of the significance and influence of the contexts in which literary texts are written and understood.

Advanced GCE Scheme of Assessment

A2 Unit F663: Drama and Poetry pre-1800

30% of the total Advanced GCE marks
2 h written paper 60 marks

Section B: Drama and Poetry pre-1800

Candidates are required to write an essay that is a comparative study of one drama and one poetry text.

Candidates are assessed on:

AO1: articulate creative, informed and relevant responses to literary texts, using appropriate terminology and concepts, and coherent, accurate written expression;

AO2: demonstrate detailed critical understanding in analysing the ways in which structure, form and language shape meanings in literary texts;

AO3: explore connections and comparisons between different literary texts, informed by interpretations of other readers;

AO4: demonstrate understanding of the significance and influence of the contexts in which literary texts are written and received.

Assessment Criteria for A2 Unit F663: *Drama and Poetry pre-1800*

Band 6 26–30 marks	AO 1	• excellent and consistently detailed understanding of texts and question; • consistently fluent, precise writing in appropriate register; • critical terminology used accurately and consistently; • well-structured, coherent and detailed argument consistently developed.
	AO 2	• well-developed and consistently detailed discussion of effects (including dramatic effects) of language, form and structure; • excellent and consistently effective use of analytical methods; • consistently effective use of quotations and references to text, critically addressed, blended into discussion.
	AO 3	• excellent and consistently detailed comparative analysis of relationships between texts; • well-informed and effective exploration of different readings of text.
	AO 4	• consistently well-developed and consistently detailed understanding of the significance and influence of contexts in which literary texts are written and understood, as appropriate to the question.
Band 5 21–25 marks	AO 1	• good and secure understanding of texts and question; • good level of coherence and accuracy in writing, in appropriate register; • critical terminology used accurately; • well-structured argument with clear line of development.
	AO 2	• developed and good level of detail in discussion of effects (including dramatic effects) of language, form and structure; • good use of analytical methods; • good use of quotations and references to text, generally critically addressed.
	AO 3	• good, clear comparative analysis of relationships between texts; • judgements informed by recognition of different readings of texts.
	AO 4	• good, clear evaluation of the significance and influence of contexts in which literary texts are written and understood, as appropriate to the question.

Band 4 **16–20** **marks**	AO 1	• competent understanding of texts and question; • clear writing in generally appropriate register; • critical terminology used appropriately; • straightforward arguments generally competently structured.
	AO 2	• generally developed discussion of effects (including dramatic effects) of language, form and structure; • competent use of analytical methods; • competent use of illustrative quotations and references to support discussion.
	AO 3	• competent comparative discussion of relationships between texts; • answer informed by some reference to different readings of texts.
	AO 4	• competent understanding of the significance and influence of contexts in which literary texts are written and understood, as appropriate to the question.
Band 3 **11–15** **marks**	AO 1	• some understanding of texts and main elements of question; • some clear writing, some inconsistencies in register; • some appropriate use of critical terminology; • some structured argument evident, lacking development and/or full illustration.
	AO 2	• some attempt to develop discussion of effects (including dramatic effects) of language, form and structure; • some attempt at using analytical methods; • some use of quotations/references as illustration.
	AO 3	• some attempt to develop comparative discussion of relationships between texts; • some awareness of different readings of texts.
	AO 4	• some understanding of the significance and influence of contexts in which literary texts are written and understood, as appropriate to the question.

Band 2 **6–10** **marks**	AO 1	• limited understanding of texts and partial attempt at question; • inconsistent writing, frequent instances of technical error, limited use of appropriate register; • limited use of critical terminology; • limited attempt to structure discussion; tendency to lose track of argument.
	AO 2	• limited discussion of effects (including dramatic effects) of language, form and structure; • descriptive or narrative comment; limited use of analytical methods; • limited or inconsistent use of quotations, uncritically presented.
	AO 3	• limited comparative discussion of relationships between texts; • limited awareness of different readings of texts.
	AO 4	• limited understanding of the significance and influence of contexts in which literary texts are written and understood, as appropriate to the question.
Band 1 **0–5** **marks**	AO 1	• very little or no relevant understanding of texts; • very inconsistent writing with persistent serious technical errors, very little or no use of appropriate register; • persistently inaccurate or no use of critical terminology; • undeveloped, very fragmentary discussion.
	AO 2	• very little relevant or no discussion of effects (including dramatic effects) of language, form and structure; • very infrequent commentary; very little or no use of analytical methods; • very few quotations (eg one or two) used (and likely to be incorrect), or no quotations used.
	AO 3	• very little or no relevant comparative discussion of relationships between texts; • very little or no relevant awareness of different readings of texts.
	AO 4	• very little reference to (and likely to be irrelevant) or no understanding of the significance and influence of contexts in which literary texts are written and understood, as appropriate to the question.

John Milton

Paradise Lost Book 1

A Note on the Text

The text is based on the first edition (1667) though I have removed all capitals except those which denote proper names (for example, *Heaven* when it means God's home rather than the sky) and God himself (for example, *the Thunderer*), all italics, and all archaic spellings and contractions of words except those which affect the metre (for example, *th'Eternal*). I have followed John Broadbent (Cambridge University Press, 1972), though much more sparingly, in adding the occasional accent where a modern pronunciation would affect metre. Punctuation has been retained (except for the addition of one or two question marks and full stops), but as Milton used commas, semi-colons, colons, and full stops in ascending order to denote the greater length of the pauses the voice should make when reading the poem aloud, do not expect them to help very much with conveying the grammar.

Paradise Lost Book I

Of Man's first disobedience, and the fruit
Of that forbidden tree, whose mortal taste
Brought death into the world, and all our woe,
With loss of Eden, till one greater Man
5 Restore us, and regain the blissful seat,
Sing heavenly Muse, that on the secret top
Of Oreb, or of Sinai, didst inspire
That shepherd who first taught the chosen seed,
In the beginning how the heavens and earth
10 Rose out of Chaos; or if Sion hill
Delight thee more, and Siloa's brook that flowed
Fast by the oracle of God: I thence
Invoke thy aid to my adventurous song,
That with no middle flight intends to soar
15 Above th'Aonian mount, while it pursues
Things unattempted yet in prose or rhyme.
And chiefly thou O Spirit, that dost prefer
Before all temples th'upright heart and pure,
Instruct me, for thou know'st; thou from the first
20 Wast present, and with mighty wings outspread
Dove-like sat'st brooding on the vast abyss
And mad'st it pregnant: what in me is dark
Illumine, what is low raise and support;
That to the highth of this great argument
25 I may assert eternal Providence,
And justify the ways of God to men.

Say first, for Heaven hides nothing from thy view
Nor the deep tract of Hell, say first what cause
Moved our grandparents in that happy state,
30 Favoured of heaven so highly, to fall off

3

From their Creator, and transgress his will
For one restraint, lords of the world besides?
Who first seduced them to that foul revolt?
Th'infernal serpent; he it was, whose guile
35   Stirred up with envy and revenge, deceived
The mother of Mankind, what time his pride
Had cast him out from Heaven, with all his host
Of rebel angels, by whose aid aspiring
To set himself in glory above his peers,
40   He trusted to have equalled the most High,
If he opposed; and with ambitious aim
Against the throne and monarchy of God
Raised impious war in heaven and battle proud
With vain attempt. Him the Almighty Power
45   Hurled headlong flaming from th'ethereal sky
With hideous ruin and combustion down
To bottomless perdition, there to dwell
In adamantine chains and penal fire,
Who durst defy the Omnipotent to arms.

50   Nine times the space that measures day and night
To mortal men, he with his horrid crew
Lay vanquished, rolling in the fiery gulf
Confounded though immortal. But his doom
Reserved him to more wrath; for now the thought
55   Both of lost happiness and lasting pain
Torments him; round he throws his baleful eyes
That witnessed huge affliction and dismay
Mixed with obdurate pride and steadfast hate:
At once as far as angels' ken he views
60   The dismal situation waste and wild,
A dungeon horrible, on all sides round
As one great furnace flamed, yet from those flames
No light, but rather darkness visible
Served only to discover sights of woe,

65 Regions of sorrow, doleful shades, where peace
And rest can never dwell, hope never comes
That comes to all; but torture without end
Still urges, and a fiery deluge, fed
With ever-burning sulphur unconsumed:
70 Such place eternal Justice had prepared
For those rebellious, here their prison ordained
In utter darkness, and their portion set
As far removed from God and light of heaven
As from the centre thrice to th'utmost pole.
75 O how unlike the place from whence they fell!
There the companions of his fall, o'erwhelmed
With floods and whirlwinds of tempestuous fire,
He soon discerns, and weltering by his side
One next himself in power, and next in crime,
80 Long after known in Palestine, and named
Beëlzebub. To whom the arch-enemy,
And thence in heaven called Satan, with bold words
Breaking the horrid silence thus began.

Satan: 'If thou beest he; but O how fallen! how changed
85 From him, who in the happy realms of light
Clothed with transcendent brightness didst outshine
Myriads though bright: if he whom mutual league,
United thoughts and counsels, equal hope,
And hazard in the glorious enterprise,
90 Joined with me once, now misery hath joined
In equal ruin: into what pit thou seest
From what highth fallen, so much the stronger proved
He with his thunder: and till then who knew
The force of those dire arms? Yet not for those
95 Nor what the potent Victor in his rage
Can else inflict, do I repent or change,
Though changed in outward lustre, that fixed mind
And high disdain, from sense of injured merit,

That with the mightiest raised me to contend,
100 And to the fierce contention brought along
Innumerable force of spirits armed
That durst dislike his reign, and me preferring,
His utmost power with adverse power opposed
In dubious battle on the plains of heaven,
105 And shook his throne. What though the field be lost?
All is not lost; th'unconquerable will,
And study of revenge, immortal hate,
And courage never to submit or yield:
And what is else not to be overcome?
110 That glory never shall his wrath or might
Extort from me. To bow and sue for grace
With suppliant knee, and deify his power
Who from the terror of this arm so late
Doubted his empire, that were low indeed,
115 That were an ignominy and shame beneath
This downfall; since by fate the strength of gods
And this empyreal substance cannot fail,
Since through experience of this great event
In arms not worse, in foresight much advanced,
120 We may with more successful hope resolve
To wage by force or guile eternal war
Irreconcilable to our grand Foe,
Who now triumphs, and in th'excess of joy
Sole reigning holds the tyranny of Heaven.'
125   So spake the apostate angel, though in pain,
Vaunting aloud, but racked with deep despair:

And him thus answered soon his bold compeer.
Beëlzebub: 'O prince, O chief of many thronèd powers
That led th'embattled seraphim to war
130 Under thy conduct, and in dreadful deeds
Fearless, endangered heaven's perpetual King;
And put to proof his high supremacy,

Whether upheld by strength, or chance, or fate;
Too well I see and rue the dire event,
135 That with sad overthrow and foul defeat
Hath lost us heaven, and all this mighty host
In horrible destruction laid thus low,
As far as gods and heavenly essences
Can perish: for the mind and spirit remains
140 Invincible, and vigour soon returns,
Though all our glory extinct, and happy state
Here swallowed up in endless misery.
But what if he our Conqueror, (whom I now
Of force believe Almighty, since no less
145 Than such could have o'erpowered such force as ours)
Have left us this our spirit and strength entire
Strongly to suffer and support our pains,
That we may so suffice his vengeful ire,
Or do him mightier service as his thralls
150 By right of war, whate'er his business be
Here in the heart of Hell to work in fire,
Or do his errands in the gloomy deep;
What can it then avail though yet we feel
Strength undiminished, or eternal being
155 To undergo eternal punishment?'

Whereto with speedy words the arch-fiend replied.
Satan: 'Fallen cherub, to be weak is miserable
Doing or suffering: but of this be sure,
To do aught good never will be our task,
160 But ever to do ill our sole delight,
As being the contrary to his high will
Whom we resist. If then his Providence
Out of our evil seek to bring forth good,
Our labour must be to pervert that end,
165 And out of good still to find means of evil;
Which oft-times may succeed, so as perhaps

Shall grieve him, if I fail not, and disturb
His inmost counsels from their destined aim.
But see the angry Victor hath recalled
170 His ministers of vengeance and pursuit
Back to the gates of heaven: the sulphurous hail
Shot after us in storm, o'erblown hath laid
The fiery surge, that from the precipice
Of heaven received us falling, and the thunder,
175 Winged with red lightning and impetuous rage,
Perhaps hath spent his shafts, and ceases now
To bellow through the vast and boundless deep.
Let us not slip th'occasion, whether scorn,
Or satiate fury yield it from our Foe.
180 Seest thou yon dreary plain, forlorn and wild,
The seat of desolation, void of light,
Save what the glimmering of these livid flames
Casts pale and dreadful? Thither let us tend
From off the tossing of these fiery waves,
185 There rest, if any rest can harbour there,
And reassembling our afflicted powers,
Consult how we may henceforth most offend
Our Enemy, our own loss how repair,
How overcome this dire calamity,
190 What reinforcement we may gain from hope,
If not what resolution from despair.'

Thus Satan talking to his nearest mate
With head up-lift above the wave, and eyes
That sparkling blazed, his other parts besides
195 Prone on the flood, extended long and large
Lay floating many a rood, in bulk as huge
As whom the fables name of monstrous size,
Titanian, or Earth-born, that warred on Jove,
Briareos or Typhon, whom the den
200 By ancient Tarsus held, or that sea-beast

Leviathan, which God of all his works
Created hugest that swim th'ocean stream:
Him haply slumbering on the Norway foam
The pilot of some small night-foundered skiff,
205   Deeming some island, oft, as seamen tell,
With fixèd anchor in his scaly rind
Moors by his side under the lea, while night
Invests the sea, and wishèd morn delays:
So stretched out huge in length the arch-fiend lay
210   Chained on the burning lake, nor ever thence
Had risen or heaved his head, but that the will
And high permission of all-ruling Heaven
Left him at large to his own dark designs,
That with reiterated crimes he might
215   Heap on himself damnation, while he sought
Evil to others, and enraged might see
How all his malice served but to bring forth
Infinite goodness, grace and mercy shown
On Man by him seduced, but on himself
220   Treble confusion, wrath and vengeance poured.
Forthwith upright he rears from off the pool
His mighty stature; on each hand the flames
Driven backward slope their pointing spires, and
     rolled
In billows leave i'th'midst a horrid vale.
225   Then with expanded wings he steers his flight
Aloft, incumbent on the dusky air
That felt unusual weight, till on dry land
He lights, if it were land that ever burned
With solid, as the lake with liquid fire;
230   And such appeared in hue, as when the force
Of subterranean wind transports a hill
Torn from Pelorus, or the shattered side
Of thundering Etna, whose combustible
And fuelled entrails thence conceiving fire,

235 Sublimed with mineral fury, aid the winds,
And leave a singèd bottom all involved
With stench and smoke: such resting found the sole
Of unblessed feet. Him followed his next mate,
Both glorying to have scaped the Stygian flood
240 As gods, and by their own recovered strength,
Not by the sufferance of supernal Power.

Satan: 'Is this the region, this the soil, the clime,'
Said then the lost archangel, 'this the seat
That we must change for Heaven, this mournful gloom
245 For that celestial light? Be it so, since he
Who now is sovereign can dispose and bid
What shall be right: farthest from him is best
Whom reason hath equalled, force hath made
supreme
Above his equals. Farewell happy fields
250 Where joy for ever dwells: hail horrors, hail
Infernal world, and thou profoundest Hell
Receive thy new possessor: one who brings
A mind not to be changed by place or time.
The mind is its own place, and in itself
255 Can make a Heaven of Hell, a Hell of Heaven.
What matter where, if I be still the same,
And what I should be, all but less than he
Whom thunder hath made greater? Here at least
We shall be free; th'Almighty hath not built
260 Here for his envy, will not drive us hence:
Here we may reign secure, and in my choice
To reign is worth ambition though in Hell:
Better to reign in Hell, than serve in Heaven.
But wherefore let we then our faithful friends
265 Th'associates and co-partners of our loss
Lie thus astonished on th'oblivious pool,
And call them not to share with us their part

In this unhappy mansion, or once more
With rallied arms to try what may be yet
270 Regained in Heaven, or what more lost in Hell?,
    So Satan spake, and him Beëlzebub
Thus answered.
Beëlzebub: 'Leader of those armies bright,
Which but th'Omnipotent none could have foiled,
If once they hear that voice, their liveliest pledge
275 Of hope in fears and dangers, heard so oft
In worst extremes, and on the perilous edge
Of battle when it raged, in all assaults
Their surest signal, they will soon resume
New courage and revive, though now they lie
280 Grovelling and prostrate on yon lake of fire,
As we erewhile, astounded and amazed,
No wonder, fallen such a pernicious highth.'

He scarce had ceased when the superior fiend
Was moving toward the shore; his ponderous shield
285 Ethereal temper, massy, large and round,
Behind him cast; the broad circumference
Hung on his shoulders like the moon, whose orb
Through optic glass the Tuscan artist views
At evening from the top of Fésolè,
290 Or in Valdarno, to descry new lands,
Rivers or mountains in her spotty globe.
His spear, to equal which the tallest pine
Hewn on Norwegian hills, to be the mast
On some great ammiral, were but a wand
295 He walked with to support uneasy steps
Over the burning marl, not like those steps
On heaven's azure, and the torrid clime
Smote on him sore besides, vaulted with fire;
Nathless he so endured, till on the beach
300 Of that inflamèd sea, he stood and called

His legions, angel forms, who lay entranced
Thick as autumnal leaves that strow the brooks
In Vallombrosa, where th'Etrurian shades
High overarched embower; or scattered sedge
305 Afloat, when with fierce winds Orion armed
Hath vexed the Red Sea coast, whose waves o'erthrew
Busiris and his Memphian chivalry,
While with perfidious hatred they pursued
The sojourners of Goshen, who beheld
310 From the safe shore their floating carcasses
And broken chariot wheels, so thick bestrown
Abject and lost lay these, covering the flood,
Under amazement of their hideous change.
He called so loud, that all the hollow deep
315 Of Hell resounded.

Satan: 'Princes, potentates,
Warriors, the flower of Heaven, once yours, now lost,
If such astonishment as this can seize
Eternal spirits; or have ye chosen this place
After the toil of battle to repose
320 Your wearied virtue, for the ease you find
To slumber here, as in the vales of Heaven?
Or in this abject posture have ye sworn
T'adore the Conqueror? who now beholds
Cherub and seraph rolling in the flood
325 With scattered arms and ensigns, till anon
His swift pursuers from Heaven gates discern
Th'advantage, and descending tread us down
Thus drooping, or with linkèd thunderbolts
Transfix us to the bottom of this gulf.
330 Awake, arise, or be for ever fallen.'

They heard, and were abashed, and up they sprung
Upon the wing, as when men wont to watch
On duty, sleeping found by whom they dread,

Rouse and bestir themselves ere well awake.
335   Nor did they not perceive the evil plight
In which they were, or the fierce pains not feel;
Yet to their general's voice they soon obeyed
Innumerable. As when the potent rod
Of Amram's son in Egypt's evil day
340   Waved round the coast, up called a pitchy cloud
Of locusts, warping on the eastern wind,
That o'er the realm of impious Pharaoh hung
Like night, and darkened all the land of Nile:
So numberless were those bad angels seen
345   Hovering on wing under the cope of Hell
'Twixt upper, nether, and surrounding fires;
Till, as a signal given, th'uplifted spear
Of their great sultan waving to direct
Their course, in even balance down they light
350   On the firm brimstone, and fill all the plain;
A multitude, like which the populous North
Poured never from her frozen loins, to pass
Rhene or the Danaw, when her barbarous sons
Came like a deluge on the South, and spread
355   Beneath Gibraltar to the Libyan sands.
Forthwith from every squadron and each band
The heads and leaders thither haste where stood
Their great commander; godlike shapes and forms
Excelling human, princely dignities,
360   And powers that erst in heaven sat on thrones;
Though of their names in heavenly records now
Be no memorial, blotted out and rased
By their rebellion, from the Books of Life.
Nor had they yet among the sons of Eve
365   Got them new names, till wandering o'er the Earth,
Through God's high sufferance for the trial of Man,
By falsities and lies the greatest part
Of Mankind they corrupted to forsake

God their creator, and th'invisible
370   Glory of him, that made them, to transform
Oft to the image of a brute, adorned
With gay religions full of pomp and gold,
And devils to adore for deities:
Then were they known to men by various names,
375   And various idols through the heathen world.

Say, Muse, their names then known, who first, who
       last,
Roused from the slumber on that fiery couch,
At their great emperor's call, as next in worth
Came singly where he stood on the bare strand,
380   While the promiscuous crowd stood yet aloof?
The chief were those who from the pit of Hell
Roaming to seek their prey on Earth, durst fix
Their seats long after next the seat of God,
Their altars by his altar, gods adored
385   Among the nations round, and durst abide
Jehovah thundering out of Sion, throned
Between the cherubim; yea, often placed
Within his sanctuary itself their shrines,
Abominations; and with cursed things
390   His holy rites, and solemn feasts profaned,
And with their darkness durst affront his light.
First Moloch, horrid king besmeared with blood
Of human sacrifice, and parents' tears,
Though for the noise of drums and timbrels loud
395   Their children's cries unheard, that passed through
       fire
To his grim idol. Him the Ammonite
Worshipped in Rabba and her watery plain,
In Argob and in Basan, to the stream
Of utmost Arnon. Nor content with such
400   Audacious neighbourhood, the wisest heart

Of Solomon he led by fraud to build
His temple right against the temple of God
On that opprobrious hill, and made his grove
The pleasant valley of Hinnom, Tophet thence
405 And black Gehenna called, the type of Hell.
Next Chemos, th'obscene dread of Moab's sons,
From Aroar to Nebo, and the wild
Of southmost Abarim; in Hesebon
And Horonaïm, Seon's realm, beyond
410 The flowery dale of Sibma clad with vines,
And Elealè to th'asphaltic pool.
Peor his other name, when he enticed
Israel in Sittim on their march from Nile,
To do him wanton rites, which cost them woe.
415 Yet thence his lustful orgies he enlarged
Even to that hill of scandal, by the grove
Of Moloch homicide, lust hard by hate;
Till good Josiah drove them thence to Hell.
With these came they, who from the bordering flood
420 Of old Euphrates to the brook that parts
Egypt from Syrian ground, had general names
Of Baälim and Ashtaroth, those male,
These feminine. For spirits when they please
Can either sex assume, or both; so soft
425 And uncompounded is their essence pure,
Not tied or manacled with joint or limb,
Nor founded on the brittle strength of bones,
Like cumbrous flesh; but in what shape they choose
Dilated or condensed, bright or obscure,
430 Can execute their airy purposes,
And works of love or enmity fulfil.
For those the race of Israel oft forsook
Their living strength, and unfrequènt left
His righteous altar, bowing lowly down
435 To bestial gods; for which their heads as low

Bowed down in battle, sunk before the spear
Of despicable foes. With these in troop
Came Astoreth, whom the Phoenicians called
Astartè, queen of heaven, with crescent horns;
440   To whose bright image nightly by the moon
Sidonian virgins paid their vows and songs,
In Sion also not unsung, where stood
Her temple on th'offensive mountain, built
By that uxorious king, whose heart though large,
445   Beguiled by fair idolatresses, fell
To idols foul. Thammuz came next behind,
Whose annual wound in Lebanon allured
The Syrian damsels to lament his fate
In amorous ditties all a summer's day,
450   While smooth Adonis from his native rock
Ran purple to the sea, supposed with blood
Of Thammuz yearly wounded: the love-tale
Infected Sion's daughters with like heat,
Whose wanton passions in the sacred porch
455   Ezekiel saw, when by the vision led
His eye surveyed the dark idolatries
Of alienated Judah. Next came one
Who mourned in earnest, when the captive Ark
Maimed his brute image, head and hands lopped off
460   In his own temple, on the grunsel edge,
Where he fell flat, and shamed his worshippers:
Dagon his name, sea monster, upward man
And downward fish: yet had his temple high
Reared in Azotus, dreaded through the coast
465   Of Palestine, in Gath and Ascalon,
And Accaron and Gaza's frontier bounds.
Him followed Rimmon, whose delightful seat
Was fair Damascus, on the fertile banks
Of Abbana and Pharphar, lucid streams.
470   He also against the house of God was bold:

A leper once he lost and gained a king,
Ahaz his sottish conqueror, whom he drew
God's altar to disparage and displace
For one of Syrian mode, whereon to burn
475   His odious offerings, and adore the gods
Whom he had vanquished. After these appeared
A crew who under names of old renown,
Osiris, Isis, Orus and their train
With monstrous shapes and sorceries abused
480   Fanatic Egypt and her priests, to seek
Their wandering gods disguised in brutish forms
Rather than human. Nor did Israel scape
Th'infection when their borrowed gold composed
The calf in Oreb: and the rebel king
485   Doubled that sin in Bethel and in Dan,
Likening his Maker to the grazèd ox,
Jehovah, who in one night when he passed
From Egypt marching, equalled with one stroke
Both her first born and all her bleating gods.
490   Belial came last, than whom a spirit more lewd
Fell not from heaven, or more gross to love
Vice for itself: to him no temple stood
Or altar smoked; yet who more oft than he
In temples and at altars, when the priest
495   Turns atheist, as did Eli's sons, who filled
With lust and violence the house of God?
In courts and palaces he also reigns
And in luxurious cities, where the noise
Of riot ascends above their loftiest towers,
500   And injury and outrage: and when night
Darkens the streets, then wander forth the sons
Of Belial, flown with insolence and wine.
Witness the streets of Sodom, and that night
In Gibeah, when the hospitable door
505   Exposed a matron to avoid worse rape.

These were the prime in order and in might;
The rest were long to tell, though far renowned,
The Ionian gods, of Javan's issue held
Gods, yet confessed later than Heaven and Earth
510   Their boasted parents; Titan Heaven's first born
With his enormous brood, and birthright seized
By younger Saturn, he from mightier Jove
His own and Rhea's son like measure found;
So Jove usurping reigned: these first in Crete
515   And Ida known, thence on the snowy top
Of cold Olympus ruled the middle air
Their highest heaven; or on the Delphian cliff,
Or in Dodona, and through all the bounds
Of Doric land; or who with Saturn old
520   Fled over Adria to th'Hesperian fields,
And o'er the Celtic roamed the utmost isles.

All these and more came flocking; but with looks
Downcast and damp, yet such wherein appeared
Obscure some glimpse of joy, to have found their chief
525   Not in despair, to have found themselves not lost
In loss itself; which on his countenance cast
Like doubtful hue: but he his wonted pride
Soon recollecting, with high words, that bore
Semblance of worth, not substance, gently raised
530   Their fainting courage, and dispelled their fears.
Then straight commands that, at the warlike sound
Of trumpets loud and clarions, be upreared
His mighty standard; that proud honour claimed
Azazel as his right, a cherub tall:
535   Who forthwith from the glittering staff unfurled
Th'imperial ensign, which full high advanced
Shone like a meteor streaming to the wind
With gems and golden lustre rich emblazed,
Seraphic arms and trophies: all the while

540 Sonorous metal blowing martial sounds:
    At which the universal host upsent
    A shout that tore Hell's concave, and beyond
    Frighted the reign of Chaos and old Night.
    All in a moment through the gloom were seen
545 Ten thousand banners rise into the air
    With orient colours waving: with them rose
    A forest huge of spears: and thronging helms
    Appeared, and serried shields in thick array
    Of depth immeasurable: anon they move
550 In perfect phalanx to the Dorian mood
    Of flutes and soft recorders; such as raised
    To highth of noblest temper heroes old
    Arming to battle, and in stead of rage
    Deliberate valour breathed, firm and unmoved
555 With dread of death to flight or foul retreat;
    Nor wanting power to mitigate and swage
    With solemn touches, troubled thoughts, and chase
    Anguish and doubt and fear and sorrow and pain
    From mortal or immortal minds. Thus they
560 Breathing united force with fixèd thought
    Moved on in silence to soft pipes that charmed
    Their painful steps o'er the burnt soil; and now
    Advanced in view they stand, a horrid front
    Of dreadful length and dazzling arms, in guise
565 Of warriors old with ordered spear and shield,
    Awaiting what command their mighty chief
    Had to impose. He through the armed files
    Darts his experienced eye, and soon traverse
    The whole battalion views, their order due,
570 Their visages and stature as of gods,
    Their number last he sums. And now his heart
    Distends with pride, and hardening in his strength
    Glories: for never since created Man,
    Met such embodied force, as named with these

575 Could merit more than that small infantry
   Warred on by cranes: though all the giant brood
   Of Phlegra with th'heroic race were joined
   That fought at Thebes and Ilium, on each side
   Mixed with auxiliar gods; and what resounds
580 In fable or romance of Uther's son
   Begirt with British and Armoric knights;
   And all who since, baptized or infidel
   Jousted in Aspramont or Montalban,
   Damasco, or Marocco, or Trebisond,
585 Or whom Biserta sent from Afric shore
   When Charlemain with all his peerage fell,
   By Fontarabbia.

        Thus far these beyond
   Compare of mortal prowess, yet observed
   Their dread commander: he above the rest
590 In shape and gesture proudly eminent
   Stood like a tower; his form had yet not lost
   All her original brightness, nor appeared
   Less than archangel ruined, and th'excess
   Of glory obscured: as when the sun new risen
595 Looks through the horizontal misty air
   Shorn of his beams, or from behind the moon
   In dim eclipse disastrous twilight sheds
   On half the nations, and with fear of change
   Perplexes monarchs. Darkened so, yet shone
600 Above them all th'archangel: but his face
   Deep scars of thunder had entrenched, and care
   Sat on his faded cheek, but under brows
   Of dauntless courage, and considerate pride
   Waiting revenge: cruel his eye, but cast
605 Signs of remorse and passion to behold
   The fellows of his crime, the followers rather
   (Far other once beheld in bliss) condemned

For ever now to have their lot in pain,
Millions of spirits for his fault amerced
610   Of Heaven, and from eternal splendours flung
For his revolt, yet faithful how they stood,
Their glory withered. As when heaven's fire
Hath scathed the forest oaks, or mountain pines,
With singèd top their stately growth though bare
615   Stands on the blasted heath. He now prepared
To speak; whereat their doubled ranks they bend
From wing to wing, and half enclose him round
With all his peers: attention held them mute.
Thrice he essayed, and thrice in spite of scorn,
620   Tears such as angels weep, burst forth: at last
Words interwove with sighs found out their way.

Satan: 'O myriads of immortal spirits, O powers
Matchless, but with th'Almighty, and that strife
Was not inglorious, though th'event was dire,
625   As this place testifies, and this dire change
Hateful to utter: but what power of mind
Foreseeing or presaging, from the depth
Of knowledge past or present, could have feared,
How such united force of gods, how such
630   As stood like these, could ever know repulse?
For who can yet believe, though after loss,
That all these puissant legions, whose exile
Hath emptied Heaven, shall fail to re-ascend
Self-raised, and repossess their native seat?
635   For me be witness all the host of Heaven,
If counsels different, or danger shunned
By me, have lost our hopes. But he who reigns
Monarch in Heaven, till then as one secure
Sat on his throne, upheld by old repute,
640   Consent or custom, and his regal state
Put forth at full, but still his strength concealed,

Which tempted our attempt, and wrought our fall.
Henceforth his might we know, and know our own
So as not either to provoke, or dread
645   New war, provoked; our better part remains
To work in close design, by fraud or guile
What force effected not: that he no less
At length from us may find, who overcomes
By force, hath overcome but half his foe.
650   Space may produce new worlds; whereof so rife
There went a fame in Heaven that he ere long
Intended to create, and therein plant
A generation, whom his choice regard
Should favour equal to the sons of Heaven:
655   Thither, if but to pry, shall be perhaps
Our first eruption, thither or elsewhere:
For this infernal pit shall never hold
Celestial spirits in bondage, nor th'abyss
Long under darkness cover. But these thoughts
660   Full counsel must mature. Peace is despaired,
For who can think submission? War then, war
Open or understood, must be resolved.'
    He spake: and to confirm his words, out-flew
Millions of flaming swords, drawn from the thighs
665   Of mighty cherubim; the sudden blaze
Far round illumined Hell; highly they raged
Against the Highest, and fierce with graspèd arms
Clashed on their sounding shields the din of war,
Hurling defiance toward the vault of heaven.

670   There stood a hill not far whose grisly top
Belched fire and rolling smoke; the rest entire
Shone with a glossy scurf, undoubted sign
That in his womb was hid metallic ore,
The work of sulphur. Thither winged with speed
675   A numerous brigad hastened. As when bands

Of pioneers with spade and pickaxe armed
Forerun the royal camp, to trench a field,
Or cast a rampart. Mammon led them on,
Mammon, the least erected spirit that fell
680   From Heaven, for even in Heaven his looks and
          thoughts
Were always downward bent, admiring more
The riches of Heaven's pavement, trodden gold,
Than aught divine or holy else enjoyed
In vision beätific: by him first
685   Men also, and by his suggestion taught,
Ransacked the centre, and with impious hands
Rifled the bowels of their mother earth
For treasures better hid. Soon had his crew
Opened into the hill a spacious wound
690   And digged out ribs of gold. Let none admire
That riches grow in Hell; that soil may best
Deserve the precious bane. And here let those
Who boast in mortal things, and wondering tell
Of Babel, and the works of Memphian kings,
695   Learn how their greatest monuments of fame,
And strength and art are easily outdone
By spirits reprobate, and in an hour
What in an age they with incessant toil
And hands innumerable scarce perform.
700   Nigh on the plain in many cells prepared,
That underneath had veins of liquid fire
Sluiced from the lake, a second multitude
With wondrous art founded the massy ore,
Severing each kind, and scummed the bullion dross:
705   A third as soon had formed within the ground
A various mould, and from the boiling cells
By strange conveyance filled each hollow nook,
As in an organ from one blast of wind
To many a row of pipes the sound-board breathes.

710   Anon out of the earth a fabric huge
            Rose like an exhalation, with the sound
            Of dulcet symphonies and voices sweet,
            Built like a temple, where pilasters round
            Were set, and Doric pillars overlaid
715   With golden architrave; nor did there want
            Cornice or frieze, with bossy sculptures graven,
            The roof was fretted gold. Not Babylon,
            Nor great Alcairo such magnificence
            Equalled in all their glories, to enshrine
720   Belus or Serapis their gods, or seat
            Their kings, when Egypt with Assyria strove,
            In wealth and luxury. Th'ascending pile
            Stood fixed her stately highth, and straight the doors
            Opening their brazen folds discover wide
725   Within, her ample spaces, o'er the smooth
            And level pavement: from the archèd roof
            Pendant by subtle magic many a row
            Of starry lamps and blazing cressets fed
            With naphtha and asphaltus yielded light
730   As from a sky. The hasty multitude
            Admiring entered, and the work some praise
            And some the architect: his hand was known
            In Heaven by many a towered structure high,
            Where sceptred angels held their residence,
735   And sat as princes, whom the supreme King
            Exalted to such power, and gave to rule,
            Each in his hierarchy, the orders bright.
            Nor was his name unheard or unadored
            In ancient Greece; and in Ausonian land
740   Men called him Mulciber; and how he fell
            From Heaven, they fabled, thrown by angry Jove
            Sheer o'er the crystal battlements: from morn
            To noon he fell, from noon to dewy eve,
            A summer's day; and with the setting sun

745 Dropped from the zenith like a falling star,
On Lemnos th'Ægean isle: thus they relate,
Erring; for he with this rebellious rout
Fell long before; nor aught availed him now
To have built in Heaven high towers; nor did he scape
750 By all his engines, but was headlong sent
With his industrious crew to build in Hell.

Meanwhile the wingèd heralds by command
Of sovereign power, with awful ceremony
And trumpets' sound throughout the host proclaim
755 A solemn council forthwith to be held
At Pandæmonium, the high capital
Of Satan and his peers: their summons called
From every band and squarèd regiment
By place or choice the worthiest; they anon
760 With hundreds and with thousands trooping came
Attended: all access was thronged, the gates
And porches wide, but chief the spacious hall
(Though like a covered field, where champions bold
Wont ride in armed, and at the soldan's chair
765 Defied the best of paynim chivalry
To mortal combat or career with lance)
Thick swarmed, both on the ground and in the air,
Brushed with the hiss of rustling wings. As bees
In spring time, when the sun with Taurus rides,
770 Pour forth their populous youth about the hive
In clusters; they among fresh dews and flowers
Fly to and fro, or on the smoothèd plank,
The suburb of their straw-built citadel,
New rubbed with balm, expatiate and confer
775 Their state affairs. So thick the airy crowd
Swarmed and were straitened; till the signal given,
Behold a wonder! they but now who seemed
In bigness to surpass Earth's giant sons

	Now less than smallest dwarfs, in narrow room
780	Throng numberless, like that pygmean race
	Beyond the Indian mount, or fairy elves,
	Whose midnight revels, by a forest side
	Or fountain some belated peasant sees,
	Or dreams he sees, while overhead the moon
785	Sits arbitress, and nearer to the Earth
	Wheels her pale course, they on their mirth and dance
	Intent, with jocund music charm his ear;
	At once with joy and fear his heart rebounds.
	Thus incorporeal spirits to smallest forms
790	Reduced their shapes immense, and were at large,
	Though without number still amidst the hall
	Of that infernal court. But far within
	And in their own dimensions like themselves
	The great seraphic lords and cherubim
795	In close recess and secret conclave sat
	A thousand demi-gods on golden seats,
	Frequent and full. After short silence then
	And summons read, the great consult began.

Notes to Paradise Lost Book I

Synopsis to Book I: the Argument

After he had published the first edition (which we are using here) Milton wrote an argument or synopsis of events to place at the beginning of each book in the second edition of 1674. As it is very stilted, I offer the following alternative:

After introducing the whole poem, which is to centre upon disobedience to God, Milton shows us Satan and his fellow rebel angels suffering the effects of their disobedience. They are lying on a lake of fire in Hell, having just been thrown out of Heaven by Christ for refusing to accept his authority and for trying to replace God the Father by their leader Lucifer, now called Satan. He is the first to recover and discusses their situation with Beëlzebub, his lieutenant. They fly to the shore from where Satan arouses his followers from the lake and musters them like an army. The leaders of the divisions are described, and they are all encouraged by Satan to continue the fight against God, and under the direction of Mammon they prepare a palace where they will debate what to do next.

Milton's Invocation: Lines 1–26

Milton starts his poem as Homer started the Classical Epic, the *Iliad* some 2000 years before, by addressing ('invoking') a Muse, a Goddess personifying artistic inspiration. Milton distinguishes his as the true *Heavenly Muse* who had dictated the Bible (which he sees as a kind of sacred poetry) to Moses and its other 'authors'. Milton sees himself as a second Moses, inspired by this exalted Muse to make his poem far surpass Classical Epic in the grandeur of its theme.

2   **mortal**   deadly.
4   **Eden**   the garden of Eden or Paradise, from where Adam and Eve were driven after they had eaten the fruit of the forbidden tree.

one greater Man   Christ, who restored us to the blissful seat of Heaven when he paid for this first sin by dying on the Cross.

6   **heavenly Muse**   see headnote above.

7   **Oreb ... Sinai**   places where *the shepherd* Moses is said to have seen God (*Exodus* 3, 19), so being inspired to write *Genesis,* which describes the beginning of the world.

10–11   **Sion hill ... Siloa's brook**   places which inspired New Testament writers; Jesus (the *oracle of God*) taught at Sion (where the Temple stood) and cured a blind man close to (*fast by*) Siloa (*John* 9).

15   **th'Aonian mount**   Helicon, the mountain sacred to the Muses (see headnote).

18   The Holy Spirit living within the temple of the body.

19   **Instruct**   main verb which, like *sing* (6), *moved* (29), and *stirred* (35), is frequently placed at the beginning of the line.

21   **Dove-like**   in *Genesis* the creative *spirit of God moved upon the face of the waters,* and the dove showed Noah that the flood was over (*Genesis* 1:8).

21   **brooding**   meditating, but also sitting like a hen on her eggs; Milton may be alluding to the ancient idea that the world was born from an egg.

22–3   Perhaps a reference to Milton's own blindness, which also introduces his constant identification of God with light and upward movement.

25–6   This is the purpose of the whole poem: to explain God's Providence, or care and plan for Mankind, which underlies the often painful *ways of God.*

The Scope of the Whole Poem: Lines 27–49

Milton now gives a brief synopsis of the story of the whole poem. First, he tells us what is to come after the events of Books I and II: the corruption of Mankind in the garden of Eden by Satan, disguised as a *serpent* (see *Genesis* 3). Then he briefly explains Satan's motivation: *envy* of Mankind's happiness, and *revenge* against God for having thrown him and his angel-supporters out of Heaven. They were punished in this way because he had led them in a rebellion against God which resulted in a war in Heaven. Note the focus on Man's *first disobedience* (I 1); Satan is only introduced because Milton wants to explain how evil entered the world.

28 **Nor** not even.

29 **grandparents** Adam and Eve, from whom the whole human species was believed to be descended.

30-1 **fall off, transgress** desert, disobey.

32 **For one restraint ... besides?** because of a single restriction (on tasting one fruit); otherwise they had command of the Earth.

33 **seduced** tempted to corruption.

34 **Th'infernal serpent** Satan, who was the immediate *cause* (28) of Adam and Eve's eating the fruit (their *revolt*), disguised as a serpent. Note the qualities here ascribed to Satan.

36 **the mother of Mankind** Eve.

36 **what time** at the time when.

37 **host** army.

38-41 Satan had previously been an angel in Heaven who tried to become supreme over other angels (*his peers*), and, using his own *host* of rebel angels, believed (*trusted*) he could *oppose* and defeat *the most High* God himself.

43 **Raised** stirred up (main verb).

44 **vain** unsuccessful.

44 **Him** Satan, object of *Hurled*.

45 **th'ethereal** Heavenly (highest part of atmosphere).

46 **ruin** falling (see *Luke* 10:18: *I beheld Satan as lightning fall from Heaven*).

47 **perdition** loss.

48 **adamantine** fabulous unbreakable mineral (see *Jude* 1:6 in Bible).

The First Description of Hell: Lines 50–83

As Milton says in the *Argument* (or synopsis)

> ... the poem hastes into the midst of things, presenting Satan with
> his angels now fallen into Hell, ... a place of utter darkness ... Here
> Satan with his angels lying on the burning lake, thunderstruck and
> astonished, after a certain space recovers.

Do you sympathize with Satan's position here? How pictorial do you find
Milton's description of Hell?

50   **Nine times**   The rebel angels fell for nine days (VI 871) like
the Titans, to whom they are frequently compared (see note
to I 197–200); they are then chained for nine days on the
burning lake, a punishment suggested by *Revelation* 20:10.

51   **horrid**   causing horror but also bristling, shaggy (because it
is associated with hair standing up; one of Milton's favourite
words).

53   **Confounded though immortal**   cast down although unable
to die. The fallen angels are made of immortal fire, but since
they sinned they can be cast down and in pain.

53–4   **doom/Reserved**   the judgement (*doom*) on him had
preserved him to suffer more of God's wrath.

56–7   **his baleful eyes/That witnessed**   his eyes, both evil and in
pain, expressed and saw the disaster.

59   **ken**   range of vision or knowledge.

64   **discover**   reveal.

65   **doleful**   sorrowful. Note the way the scenery suggests
emotions.

66–7   **hope never comes/That comes to all**   perhaps echoing the
words inscribed above the gate of Dante's Hell: *All hope
abandon ye who enter here.*

68   **urges**   drives on (the sense of the Latin *urgeo*).

69   **sulphur**   brimstone, a corrosive chemical traditionally
associated with Hell, which burns here without being used
up (*unconsumed*).

71   **ordained**   ordered, prepared.

72   **portion**   place, fate.

73–4   The distance from Hell to Heaven is three times the distance from the centre of the Earth to the outermost orbit of the stars. As in line 50, Milton's calculations are based on the mystical number 3.

75   **unlike**   the fallen angels will try to make it more like Heaven.

78   **discerns**   makes out in the gloom.

78   **weltering**   wallowing helplessly.

81   **Beëlzebub**   'Lord of the Flies', and called 'Prince of the Demons' in *Mark* 3:22 (which is set in Palestine). He is Satan's second-in-command.

81   **arch-enemy**   the supreme enemy. *Enemy* is the principal meaning of the name *Satan*, though Satan frequently tries to apply it to God (for example, I 122).

Satan's First Speech: Lines 84–126

These lines introduce us to two sides of Satan's character: is he the noble and suffering hero standing firm against overwhelming odds, or the deceitful politician disguising his failure from his closest friend? He is already taking control of the angels' future, for he rejects some possible options (for example, 108, 111), and is only questioning whether to use *force* or *guile* in his continued war against God. This will be debated from II 41. The main points he makes are reinforced by Beëlzebub. Make a list of the ways he characterizes God (for example, *potent Victor in his rage* [95]); how far do these names help him to excuse his own failure?

84–94   **If thou beest he ...**   if you really are Beëlzebub, whom Satan says *misery hath joined* (main verb, 90) to him now, since God surprisingly proved stronger than them.

85–7   Satan used to be called Lucifer, 'light-bearer', and presumably Beëlzebub was nearly as bright in Heaven (the *happy realms of light*) if he shone brighter than the *myriads* (vast numbers) there.

87   **if he whom mutual league**   if you are really he who once joined (90) in alliance with me (but was it really *mutual?*) to help each other in the *glorious enterprise* (89) to overthrow God.

92   **highth**   height. Milton's spelling intensifies the highness.

93   **thunder**   the *ten thousand thunders* of VI 836 with which Jesus cast out the rebel angels (described at 94 as *dire arms*).

94	**dire** terrible.
94–104	Fear will not cause Satan to *repent or change* (main verbs, 96) the mind that fought against God, because his pride (*disdain*) and sense *of injured merit* (98) persists. Satan was provoked to rebel by God's promotion of Jesus over himself (V 662), and claims that his fellow rebels would have preferred him to the tyrants, God and Jesus.
95	**potent** powerful.
99–100	**contend, contention** oppose, opposition.
102	**durst** dared to.
104	**dubious** uncertain (but was it really uncertain?).
105	**field** battle.
109	'and what else cannot be overcome?'
111–16	Satan anticipates his soliloquy in Bk IV here by saying it would indeed be ignoble to ask God for forgiveness on bended knee, since God (the *who* of 113) had so recently been afraid of him.
112	**deify** make divine (ironic, as God *is* divine).
115	**ignominy** disgrace.
116–21	**fate** (a power Satan prefers to God) ensures that the angelic substance of *gods* (his name for the angels) cannot die, and as they will have improved in experience, so they may *with more successful hope* (120), continue the war with God, using either *force* or *guile*.
117	**empyreal substance** the pure fire out of which the highest heaven is made.
118	**event** outcome.
119	**In arms ... advanced** our weapons are no worse and our understanding of the possible outcome is much better.
122	**Foe** see note to I 81.
126	**Vaunting** boasting. This line sums up Satan's two sides.

Beëlzebub's First Speech: Lines 127–55

We discover here something of Beëlzebub's character and his relationship with Satan. See if you can find the following ideas expressed in both this speech and Satan's:

- a preference for seeing *Fate* or *Chance* as the supreme power
- the claim that God's victory was solely one of *strength*
- reliance on the immortality of their *heavenly essences*
- the belief that the mind can remain unchanged.

However, as Beëlzebub continues to speak, his view of the situation begins to differ from Satan's, particularly with regard to God's power. Can you see this happen? Once again it is worth listing the ways in which God is described.

128–42   Another very long and complex sentence; having addressed Satan for six lines, Beëlzebub reaches his main point at 134 (main verbs *see* and *rue*).

128   **throned powers**   rulers in the hierarchy of angels. Heaven is organized like an army.

129   **th'embattled seraphim**   armed angels (the *seraphim* were the second highest rank).

130   **conduct**   leadership (Latin *duco* I lead).

132   **his**   God's.

134   **rue**   regret.

138   **heavenly essences**   another way of referring to the *empyreal substance* explained in note to I 117.

140   **vigour**   physical strength. Beëlzebub here takes pride in their returning strength, but begins at 146 to wonder why it is returning. For the answer see note to 210–13 below.

141   **glory extinct**   their brightness has been extinguished (see line 97).

144   **Of force**   perforce, by necessity.

143–52   Beëlzebub is afraid that their returning strength will enable them to endure or *support* increased torture, or even to perform God's *errands* (as perhaps they will; see note to I 210–13). What does this tell you about his attitude to God?

146   **entire**   undamaged.

148   **suffice his vengeful ire**   satisfy his wrathful and sadistic passion for revenge.

149–50   **thralls/By right of war**   contemporary prisoners of war could, in theory, be made the slaves (*thralls*) of the conquerors.

153   **avail**   benefit.

Satan's Returning Decision and Freedom: Lines 156–91

Satan's reply begins to explain why and how he will continue his opposition to God. Lines 162–8 should be read in conjunction with 211–20, which states God's counter-policy. What does Satan's policy suggest to you? Is it childish? spiteful? heroic in the face of overwhelming odds? What does it tell you about Satan's feeling for God?

157   **Fallen cherub**   Beëlzebub, whom Satan is addressing.

157–8   **weak is miserable / Doing or suffering**   This is one of a number of places where a contrast can be drawn between Satan and Christ, who did not despise weakness. Doing/suffering (or active/passive) represents the contrasting types of human behaviour.

159   **aught**   anything.

162–8   God's caring plan for creation (his *Providence*), explained by Milton I 211–20 will indeed seek *out of our evil ... to bring forth good*. Satan plans to *pervert that end* by frustrating God wherever possible in order to *grieve him* and *disturb* his plans (*inmost counsels*).

169–70   **angry Victor**   God, as Satan presents him, for God is in fact mercifully calling back the angelic pursuers, who are therefore not acting as agents (*ministers*) of vengeance at all.

171–3   **sulphurous hail ... o'erblown hath laid / The fiery surge** the sulphur-rain that was *shot after us* has blown itself out, so that the lake of fire (*fiery surge*) is now calm (*laid*). The weather is improving.

175–6   This suggests a cartoon picture, in which the thunderbolts have lightning wings. Satan hopes it has run out of missiles (*spent his shafts*), thus concealing again the fact that God must be easing their torments on purpose.

176   **his**   its (a relatively new word which Milton avoids).

177   **bellow ... boundless deep**   to resonate through Hell (the open vowels echo the meaning).

178   **slip**   miss. What does this tell you of Satan's character?

178–9   **scorn,/Or satiate fury**   Satan calls God's mercy *scorn* and suggests that his sadistic appetite is simply satisfied (*satiate*) for the moment.

180   **dreary plain**   Satan chooses this plain, which is described in emotional as well as physical terms, as the assembly ground for his troops.

181   **seat**   place.

181   **void**   empty.

182   **save**   except.

182   **livid**   bluish leaden colour.

183   **Thither ... tend**   Let us go there.

185   **rest**   Hell is characterized by change and restlessness.

187   **Consult**   main verb at beginning of line. But is Satan really going to consult his fellow angels? What decisions must he already have made to be now consulting on the issues which are outlined here?

189   **dire**   terrible.

190   **reinforcement**   encouragement.

191   **despair**   emphasized by rhyme with *repair* (188). Why is this passion so appropriate to Satan and to Hell, and how is it related to *hope* (190)?

First Description of Satan: Lines 192–241

This passage includes the first **epic similes,** elaborate comparisons usually introduced by *As* and completed by *So*. By looking at all the features which Satan has in common with the Titans, with Leviathan, or with a volcano, you can uncover what Milton is telling us about Satan apart from the fact that he is very big.

Milton also confronts here the central problem of why God allowed Satan to exist at all, let alone to have his freedom (*Left him at large*, 213). The principal answer given here is that this policy would ultimately allow God to show a much greater *grace* when he redeems the world by the sacrifice of Christ.

193–5   **up-lift ... Prone**   head lifted up, body lying flat. What does this position suggest to you? Compare it with the next images of Satan rearing up and then flying to land (221, 225).

196   **rood**   rod, an ancient unit of measurement, equal to about five metres.

197–200   As introduces the first epic simile, comparing Satan to *Titanian ... Briareos or Typhon*, two giant-monsters of the Titan race; Briareos had 100 arms, Typhon (who lived at *Tarsus*) 100 heads. The Titans deposed their father-king (Uranus), and later their new king (Saturn) was himself deposed by his son, Zeus. See I 508–14.

200–8   **Leviathan**   enormous Biblical sea-monster generally identified with the whale, and to which Milton attaches the Scandinavian (and *Arabian Nights*) fairy tale of a monster as big as an island, which deceives sailors into mooring to its hide (*rind*) before swimming away with them. The sentence-structure goes: *the pilot* (subject) *Moors* (main verb at beginning of line) by *Him* (= Leviathan) while he is *slumbering* (203).

203   **haply**   by chance.

204   **night-foundered skiff**   a small boat disabled and leaking at night. Satan is often associated with night and the sea.

205   **Deeming**   believing.

207   **under the lea**   on the side sheltered from the wind.

208   **Invests**   clothes.

209   **So**   marks the end of these epic similes.

210–13   **nor ever thence/Had risen**   nor would ever have risen from there. Milton here intrudes his own voice to answer Beëlzebub's question at 143–52 and Satan's boast at 162–68; Milton follows St. Augustine in the belief that ultimately everything which happens is within God's plan or *Providence*.

213   **at large**   at liberty.

214   **reiterated**   repeated.

216   **enraged**   filled with rage.

219   **On Man by him seduced**   God's *grace* will be shown to man because he was induced to commit sin (*seduced*) by Satan.

221   **Forthwith**   straight away.

221   **rears**   raises, lifts (his *mighty stature*).

222–4   Satan's sudden movement creates a trough bristling with fire (*horrid vale*) and surrounded by flames sloping away from it.

226   **incumbent**   leaning.

228 **He lights**   he alights, touches down, on the burning 'land' which surrounds the lake of fire.

230–7   This third epic simile appears to elaborate on Satan's *hue* (colour, 230) but is really a comparison of his movement with that of the torn mountainsides which Milton imagines would fly through the air when the Sicilian volcanoes *Pelorus* and *Etna* erupt. Milton had visited Sicily, but look for the words which suggest not eruption so much as an industrial explosion, or the belching and farting demons of Hieronymous Bosch.

231 **subterranean wind**   underground force (but why *wind?*).

233–4   **combustible … Sublimed**   The inflammable fuel in the centre of the mountain is ignited by the underground *wind* and immediately becomes flame and vapour.

236–7   **singed bottom all involved**   the burnt floor, wrapped in *stench and smoke* (again note the body-language) where the mountainside had been.

237 **such resting**   ironic, as there is no rest in Hell (see I 66).

239 **glorying to have scaped**   triumphant in their escape, as at 1240–1.

239 **Stygian flood**   Hellish lake (alluding to the Greek Underworld river, the Styx).

241 **sufferance of supernal Power**   the permission of almighty Power (referring to line 212 above).

Satan Takes Possession of his New Kingdom: Lines 242–82

Here, as so often, Satan seems to see the truth only to manipulate it. How does he convey his sense of a real loss, but immediately excuse or justify himself, or in other ways change the facts? How far do you agree with Satan's assertion that *Here at least/We shall be free* (258–9)? This is also one of several passages which 'internalize Hell' by suggesting it is essentially within the mind. This exchange with Beëlzebub displays not only Satan's concern for his *associates and co-partners* (265), but also (according to the flattering Beëlzebub) his power over them. Do you think he is misusing it here?

242   **clime**   climate.

244–5   **gloom ... light**   it shows that Satan is still partly good that he recognizes the essential superiority of light over darkness; Mammon confuses the distinction II 262–8.

246–7   **dispose and bid/What shall be right**   Satan asserts that God wilfully arranges and decides what is right (rather than acting righteously because he is good).

248   Satan claims equality with God in all but strength; compare I 92, 133, 258.

253   **A mind not to be changed**   This is both heroic and deeply ironic; changelessness is an attribute of Heaven only, and Satan changes and deteriorates before our eyes; compare this speech with the spitefulness and lies of his thoughts in Bk II.

254–5   The truth that *the mind is its own place* explains how Satan could invent Sin in Heaven, and later suggests true hope for Adam, who *is* told he *shalt possess/A Paradise within thee happier far* than the one he lost (XII 586–7).

258   **thunder**   see note to I 93.

259   **free**   suggests the ideals of the Commonwealth.

261   **we may reign secure**   how do you see the plural *we* here?

262   **worth ambition**   worth being ambitious for.

263   **Better to reign in Hell**   This sounds Classically heroic; Caesar supposedly said 'I would rather be first in this miserable village than second in Rome.' (Plutarch *Life* XI 2, or see Homer's *Odyssey* XI 489–91). But in a religious context it suggests a 'service to sin' (*Romans* 6) rather than the 'perfect freedom' of service to God (*Book of Common Prayer*). Mammon later describes what he thinks it would be like to *serve in Heaven*.

266   **astonished**   stunned

266   **th'oblivious pool**   they lie forgetful on the lake of fire.

267–9   **call them not ... to try**   follows *wherefore* of 264: 'why do we not call them to try once more?'

268   **mansion**   dwelling (where they *manent*, from *manere* (Latin) meaning to remain).

269   **rallied arms**   reassembled weapons.

273   **Which but ... foiled**   which none but the All-powerful could have prevented from winning.

274   **liveliest pledge**   most vital promise. Beëlzebub claims that
         Satan's voice alone rallies the angels in tight corners (*worst*
         extremes, perilous edge/Of battle, all assaults, 276–7).

278   **resume**   main verb, following *If* (274): 'they will become
         brave again.'

280   **yon**   yonder.

281   **erewhile**   previously.

282   **pernicious highth**   deadly height.

Second Description of Satan and His Awakening of the Fallen Angels: Lines 283–330

This passage, with its Classical and Biblical epic similes and its wonderful speech, is one of the most heroic in the poem. Yet there may be other elements in the description of Satan and the angels, or in his address to them, which give you a more negative impression. Are the angels the victims of Satan's egotism, or are they being helped by him to recover their self-esteem and ability to act? The passage also introduces the story of the Flight from Egypt by Moses and the Jewish people, which is the source of many comparisons in I and II.

283   **superior fiend**   Satan now walks to the *shore* of the burning
         lake, from where he had flown to the *dreary plain* (180).

284–6 **ponderous shield … Behind him cast**   he carried his
         weighty shield, hardened in heavenly fire (*Ethereal temper*),
         over his shoulder. Achilles, the hero of Homer's *Iliad*, has a
         similarly mighty shield which is described at length.

287–91 Epic simile introduced by *like* comparing the shield to the
         moon. Milton visited the then blind *Tuscan artist*, or
         astronomer, Galileo, in Florence (situated in Valdarno in
         Tuscany) in 1638, and was probably allowed to view the
         moon through the telescope (*optic glass*), which Galileo was
         believed to have invented, from the nearby hill at *Fésolè*
         (Fiesole).

292–5 Compared to his spear, the tallest pine cut (*hewn*) in Norway
         to be a mast for an *ammiral* (flagship) would have looked like

a small stick (*wand* – no magical connotations). The size-shifting in these two similes is significant. The moon is bigger than the shield; the tree is smaller than the spear. It is as if Milton is using the telescope at both ends to create a dream-like effect.

296   **marl**   earth.

297   **azure**   blue.

297–8   **torrid clime ... vaulted with fire**   Satan is painfully affected by the scorchingly hot climate under the fiery roof of Hell.

299   **Nathless**   nevertheless.

302   **autumnal leaves**   The first of three epic similes for the fallen angels. They lie stunned (*entranced*), as thick as the golden leaves on the valley floor at *Vallombrosa* (or 'valley of shadows') in Etruria or Tuscany. Vergil also compares the dead to fallen leaves.

304   **scattered sedge**   the angels are thrown about like water-weed after a storm (associated with the appearance of the star-constellation *Orion*, who is *armed* with a sword).

307   **Busiris and his Memphian chivalry**   Pharaoh and the Egyptian troops (who drowned when Moses closed the waters of the Red Sea on them; *Exodus* 14).

308   **perfidious hatred**   treacherous hostility; the Egyptians, like Satan's army, broke their word to God (to let the Jews leave).

309   **sojourners of Goshen**   the Jews, who journeyed to Goshen on the far side of the Nile.

313   **amazement**   shock, bewilderment; also suggests wandering in a maze.

315–6   **Princes, potentates**   As usual, Satan begins his speech with a flattering **exordium** or address. What emotions does Satan appeal to in this speech?

319–20   **to repose / Your wearied virtue**   one of several sarcastic taunts (continuing until 325); do you think it would be better or worse if Satan apologized for the defeat?

322–3   **abject, adore**   the assonance on *a* links the two words, suggesting one has to be thrown down (*abject*) to worship.

324   **Cherub and seraph**   angelic beings.

325   **anon**   soon. Satan is alerting them to immediate danger.

325	**arms and ensigns** weapons and flags.
326–7	**discern/Th'advantage** see that we are at their mercy.
328	**linked thunderbolts** By taking the 'bolts' literally, Milton suggests chains made of thunder.
330	**Awake, arise** note the arousing rhythm of this line.

The Fallen Angels Rally and Assemble before Satan: Lines 331–75

The angels seem to feel guilty (*abashed, found by whom they dread*); is this appropriate? The epic similes which describe them concentrate on their immense numbers, and yet comparisons with *locusts* and barbarian hordes from the *frozen loins* of the North, diminish our respect for them. Milton then introduces the next substantial section of the poem, by explaining he will call the fallen angels by the *new names* of the pagan gods which they supposedly later became according to one tradition; can Milton possibly believe this to be literally true?

335–6	There are two double negatives here which cancel each other out, so that the angels do *perceive their plight* and *feel* their *pains*.
338–44	An epic simile comparing the fallen angels to the plague of locusts which Moses (*Amram's son*) called up by his supernaturally powerful (*potent*) rod to help persuade the *impious Pharaoh* to let the Jews go (*Exodus* 6:20, 10:12–15). Can you think of other points of comparison, besides their being *numberless*, between the fallen angels and a mass of insects which darken the sky, and then eat all the crops?
340	**pitchy** black.
341	**warping** whirling through the air like snow.
342	**impious** irreligious (both because Pharaoh is a pagan, and because he breaks his oath to the Jews and their God).
345	**cope** canopy.
346	**nether** lower.
348	**sultan** despot.

349   **in even balance down they light**   they alight in an ordered formation (at a signal from Satan's spear).

351–5   An epic simile comparing the angels to the *multitude* of barbarian invaders whom Machiavelli had described coming from the lands north of the Rhine and Danube (*Rhene or the Danaw*) to overturn the Roman Empire as far south as North Africa (the *Libyan sands*).

352   **frozen loins**   cold womb; perhaps rather extreme language for North Germany, but it is the first of a series of images suggesting 'false creativity' or sterility.

357   **the heads and leaders thither haste**   The leaders of each division of Satan's army advance quickly to be reviewed.

359   **princely dignities**   of royal status.

360   **erst**   before.

361–3   **their names ... and rased ... from the Books of Life.**   The names they had in Heaven, such as Lucifer (which was Satan's), have been deleted from God's book of the blessed (see *Revelation* 21:27).

364   **sons of Eve**   derogatory term for Mankind (because Eve was faithless).

365   **new names**   see headnote.

366   **God's high sufferance for the trial of Man**   God's allowance of liberty to the fallen angels so they can test Mankind; see I 213.

369–70   **th'invisible ... to transform**   The fallen angels, by telling lies (*falsities*, 367) persuade men to worship them in the form of idols decorated with tinsel (*gay religions*, 372), instead of the invisible true God. Milton, as a Protestant, may be thinking of the Catholics as well as pagans here.

The Parade of Angels as Pagan Gods: Lines 376–521

A new invocation *Say Muse* (see note to 1 6) alerts us to a new episode, a catalogue of heroes typical of Classical epic. As explained in the previous headnote, Milton is using an old tradition that *long after* the fall of the angels from Heaven, they were worshipped on Earth as the pagan gods. Satan's commanders are a select group of these: the pagan gods chosen for worship by the Jewish kings themselves, who had temples near or even on Mount Sion, where the Temple to Jehovah stood (*I Kings* 11:7–9; *II Kings* 18:10–18; 21:1–5). The implication is that if even God's chosen people, the Jews, chose to follow pagan gods and the vices they represent, then Christians nowadays might also be tempted to follow the 'gods' of violence, self-indulgence, materialism, and so forth. Satan's commanders are, therefore, the representatives not of heroic but of degraded human qualities. As you read, keep thinking of the modern equivalents.

The whole passage (like its parallel in *Nativity Ode* 197–228) exhibits Milton's knowledge of Hebrew and Jewish scholarship, but maybe the place-names are chosen as much for their music as their authenticity. As it is is very long, I have divided it into sub-sections **[a)-f)]** after a brief introductory section.

377	**fiery couch**	the burning lake.
379	**Came singly**	each named leader comes before Satan in the parade in order of importance (*worth*, 378).
379	**strand**	beach.
380	**promiscuous**	undiscriminated.
382	**prey**	human beings to tempt and corrupt.
385	**durst abide**	dared endure (by being so close).
386–7	**throned/Between the cherubim**	There were gold cherubim at each end of the sacred Ark of the Covenant in the Temple which was on Mount *Sion* (*Psalm* 80:1).
388	**Within his sanctuary**	Altars to pagan gods were actually set up within the Temple itself (see *II Kings* 21:1–5).
389	**Abominations**	pagan gods (the word used in the Authorized Version quoted in the next headnote).
391	**affront**	insult.

a) Moloch and Chemos: Lines 392–418

Milton puts at the front the gods whose temples were the greatest *affront* (391) to *Jehovah*, the true God. In *Kings* 11:7–9 Solomon (under his wives' influence, of course) built *a high place for Chemos, the abomination* of Moab, *in the hill that is before Jerusalem, and for Moloch, the abomination of the children of Ammon. And likewise did he for all his foreign wives, who burned incense and sacrificed unto their gods. And the Lord was angry with Solomon.* What vices do these two gods suggest to you?

392   **Moloch**   Milton follows the historian Sandys in describing him as an idol with a furnace in his chest in which children were burned as sacrifices while priests drowned their cries *with the continual clang of trumpets and timbrels* (tambourines). (See *A Relation of a Journey* (1637), Fowler edition of *P.L.*)

392   **horrid king**   horrific king (*Moloch* means *king*).

396   **Ammonite**   followers of Moloch living in *Rabba*, the *city of waters* (*II Samuel* 12:27) and in Argob and Basan, which were also in Judah (*Judges* 11:13).

400   **Audacious neighbourhood**   presumptuous position (in Judah).

403   **opprobrious hill**   (*hill of scandal* at 416) the shameful idol-covered hill *before Jerusalem* (see headnote a), later the Mount of Olives, *against* (opposite) Jehovah's Temple on Mount Sion.

404–5   The valley that divided these hills was therefore discredited, lost the name *Hinnon*, and acquired the shameful names *Tophet* and *Gehenna* which were associated with Hell.

406   **Chemos**   the Moabite god; see headnote a) and *Numbers* 21:29.

407–11   These Biblical place-names, like *Sittim* (413) were associated with the Moabites.

411   **th'asphaltic pool**   the Dead Sea, which contains bitumens (inflammable minerals), such as asphalt.

412   **Peor**   Baal-Peor was another name for Chemos, whom the Jews briefly worshipped during their escape from Egypt.

414–15   **wanton rites, lustful orgies**   sexual licence associated with Chemos/Peor.

414   **cost them woe**   The Jews who worshipped Peor were punished by a plague (*woe*); see *Numbers* 25:1–9.

416   **hill of scandal**   see note to I 403.

417   **lust hard by hate**   The two temples, to Moloch and to Chemos, like these vices they represent, were very close (*hard by*) to each other.

418   **Josiah**   the king who destroyed the two temples and turned the valley to a rubbish dump (*II Kings* 23:13).

b) Baalim, Ashtaroth, and Thammuz: Lines 419–56

Milton now considers the sun-gods *Baalim* (plural of the generalized name Baal, 'Lord'), and the moon-goddess *Ashtareth* (plural *Ashtoreth*) who loved the beautiful youth *Thammuz*. They were worshipped in the area stretching from Canaan up as far as the Euphrates, and the cult of Thammuz in particular was associated with excessive emotionalism. Is Milton raising the question of which vices are 'gender-specific'? But if so, why is he so insistent that neither evil nor good spirits have any particular name, number, gender or shape (421–31)? Where in Book I do we see the angels change shape or size, becoming *dilated* or *condensed*?

420   **brook**   the river Besor (I *Samuel* 30:10).

423   **spirits**   good as well as bad angels.

425   **essence**   the *quintessence* (III 716) or *empyreal substance* (I 117) from which the angels are made. As Raphael explains in more detail in VIII 620–9 it is so pure (*uncompounded*) that angels can flow into one another when making love.

426   **manacled**   As Man, unlike the angels, is a mixture of soul and body, his hands (*mains*) and other limbs act as handcuffs (*manacles*) chaining the free spirit inside the body.

427   **founded on the brittle strength**   based on fragile physical strength (as opposed to the *living strength* of God (433; see *I Samuel* 15:29).

431   **love or enmity**   depending on whether they are good or evil spirits.

432–7   **For those**   for Baal and Ashtareth (see *Judges* 2:13–14 where the Jews *forsook the Lord, and served Baal and Ashtareth ... And the Lord delivered them into the hands of spoilers ... and enemies.*)

435   **bestial**   beast-like in form or nature (as *brutish* at I 481).

438–9   **Astoreth ... Astartè**   The moon, here a horned goddess, is often associated with women (who have a monthly cycle). Phoenecia is on the coast of Syria and contains the city of Sidon (hence *Sidonian*).

442–3 **Sion ... offensive mountain** see note to 403 above.

444 **uxorious** over-fond of his (700) wives (see headnote a).

446 **Thammuz** The youth known in Greece as *Adonis*, whom *Astarte* loved and revived from death; this was celebrated annually as part of a fertility cult in Lebanon in late summer, when the Adonis river runs red with earth, suggesting his blood running from the boar-wound which had killed him (*yearly wounded*, 452).

453 **Infected Sion's daughters** The Jewish women (*Sions daughters*) also began to express sorrow (*like heat*) for Thammuz, and this led to sexual rites which Ezekiel saw in a vision (*Ezekiel* 8:14). What is the connection which Milton seems to be making between sorrow and sex here?

457 **alienated Judah** the Jews in exile in Babylon.

c) Dagon and Rimmon: Lines 457–76

The Philistines of Palestine (which contained the cities *Azotus*, *Gath*, *Ascalon*, *Accaron*, and *Gaza*) captured the holy Ark of the Jews, their traditional enemies, and put it in the temple of Dagon. The next morning the idol had lost its human head and hands; only its fish-tail was left (*I Samuel* 5:1–5). Rimmon was a Damascan god whom the Jewish king Ahaz worshipped (so that he *gained a king*).

459 **Maimed** see headnote c).

460 **grunsel** threshold.

467 **Him followed** came after Dagon (who presumably jumps along on his tail).

467–71 Rimmon's temple (*delightful seat*) was in Damascus on the confluence of the rivers *Abbana* and *Pharphar*, in which the leper Naaman said he would prefer to bathe, after Elisha told him to bathe in the Jordan – which he eventually did and was cured (*II Kings* 5:1–19) and so *lost* to Rimmon's worship.

472 **Ahaz his sottish conqueror** The foolish Ahaz who displaced one of Jehovah's altars in the Temple by a copy of Rimmon's altar, although he had *vanquished* (476) Damascas and so should have appreciated the superiority of Jehovah (see *II Kings* 16:10–15).

d) The Egyptian Gods: Lines 476–89

Milton identifies the Golden Calf worshipped by the Jews in *Oreb* (*Exodus* 32:1–6) with the *brutish* bovine gods of Egypt, from where they were escaping. Thus, like the gods he has mentioned, these too represent a false choice made by the 'people of God' in the Bible. Since Man is distinguished from beasts by his soul and his reason, to choose to worship a beast is to deliberately degenerate. What modern equivalent can you think of for such a false choice?

478   **Osiris, Isis, Orus**   *Osiris* was worshipped as a bull, *Isis* had cow's horns, and *Orus* was their calf-child.

479–80   **abused/Fanatic Egypt**   deceived the extremist priests of Egypt. The fallen angels took animal shapes (*monstrous ... brutish*) or heads, and induced the Egyptians to worship them.

481   **wandering gods**   Isis wandered the world seeking the parts of Osiris' body.

481   **brutish forms**   see headnote d) and note to I 435.

483   **Th'infection**   see note to 453 above.

483   **borrowed**   the priest Aaron took the golden earrings of the Jews to make the golden calf; see headnote d).

484   **rebel king**   Jeroboam, who later set up two (*doubled*) golden calves, in *Bethel* and *Dan* in Sumaria (*I Kings* 12:20–29). These, like the original Golden Calf, were said to have delivered the Jews from Egypt (*Psalm* 106:20).

487–9   On the 'Passover' night God *passed* over the Jewish houses, but made the Egyptian first-born as dead (*equalled*) as their own gods; this *stroke* was the real reason for the Jews' deliverance from Egypt (*Exodus* 12:29–33).

489   **bleating**   cry of calves as well as sheep.

e) Belial: Lines 490–505

Belial has no altar because he was not really a distinct god in the Bible; the phrase *the sons/Of Belial* (501–2) seems to represent people enslaved to a group of vices rather than a specific idol. Using the Biblical references Milton invents a new character, and gives him the vices of the rich in *courts and palaces*: atheism, gluttony, luxury, lust, violence, drunkenness, and sodomy.

490   **last**   of the named gods/angels.

491   **gross**   blatant.

495   **Eli's sons**   sons of the priest who preferred to eat rather than to sacrifice holy animals (*I Samuel* 2:12–17), suggesting the vice of greed.

500   **injury and outrage**   insults and violation of others' rights.

500   **night**   as usual (for example, I 440 above) Milton associates vice with darkness.

502   **flown**   'high flown' or 'high' in the modern sense.

503–5   **Sodom, Gibeah**   In both cities a woman is offered to the *sons of Belial* by a *hospitable* Jew wishing to protect male guests from homosexual (*worse*) rape (*Genesis* 19:4–11; *Judges* 19: 22–28).

f) The Classical Gods: Lines 506–21

Having named the Biblical gods, Milton describes the Classical gods much more briefly, because the Jews never followed them. Why also might he not not want to associate them with vice or betrayal?

508   **Ionian Gods**   the Olympian Gods.

508   **Javan**   a descendant of Noah and the supposed ancestor of the Greek race (*Genesis* 10:2).

508   **held**   believed.

509–10   **Gods ... first born**   they admitted themselves that they were younger than Uranus (*Heaven*) and Ge (*Earth*), whom they proudly claimed as their great-grandparents (their parents were the Titans).

510–14   **Saturn**   the youngest of the Titans, said here to be the children (*brood*) of Uranus' eldest son, *Titan*. Saturn deposed his father and was himself deposed in the same way (*like measure*) by Zeus (*Jove*), the son he had by *Rhea*. These *usurping* acts repeat the sin of Satan; see note to I 196–200.

514–15   **Crete/And Ida**   Mount Ida in Crete was believed to be the birthplace of Zeus (and tourists are even shown his bath).

516   **Olympus**   The gods supposedly inhabited the highest mountain in Greece, Olympus, which is always snow-covered.

516–17   **middle air ... heaven**   the air at the level of mountain tops which is the part inhabited by spirits who cannot reach the *empyrean* (God's Heaven).

517–19   **Delphi, Dodona**   places in Greece (*Doric land*) where the Classical gods were *renowned* (507) for oracles. Note the dreamy effect of the alliteration.

519   **or who**   further examples of *The rest* (507), this time from outside Greece.

519–21   After being deposed, Saturn fled over the Adriatic Sea (*Adria*) to Italy (*th'Hesperian fields*) and France (*Celtic*) to Britain (*utmost isles*) where he may still lie asleep on Anglesey.

Satan Comforts and Marshals the Fallen Angels: Lines 522–87

Satan seems here to show genuine concern for his army, and he encourages them by calling them to arms, though as usual there are words which might undermine this positive impression. Should we be impressed by him? Should we feel an increasing admiration for the angels? They do seem to be trying to recover from their *abject posture* on the burning lake, when their arms lay *scattered* around them (see I 322, 325). There are a number of upward-moving (for example *upreared, upsent*) and brightening (*meteor, lustre*) words associated with them, but perhaps this recovery should be seen as superficial and temporary. Why does Milton compare them to armies which seem more fictional than real – first the Classical soldiers dancing to *Dorian* music, and then the armies of Italian epics and English and French Romances? Should we be thinking of the heroic qualities and vast spectacle of such armies, or of their unreality?

523   **such wherein**   such *looks* (522) in which.

525   **despair**   See note to I 126.

527   **like doubtful hue**   the same ambiguous expression.

527–8   **wonted pride/Soon recollecting**   quickly summoning up his usual pride.

529   **Semblance … not substance**   the appearance of value, not the reality.

529–30   What do *gently* and *dispelled* tell you about Satan? Why does

Milton feel he must interpose his own voice to discredit Satan's words as having *Semblance of worth, not substance* (they only seemed valuable and true)?

531   **straight**   immediately.

532   **clarions**   shrill military trumpets.

533–6   **standard ... imperial ensign**   Satan's personal flag.

534   **Azazel**   one of Satan's four standard bearers according to Jewish 'cabbalistic' (occult) writings, in which Milton was keenly interested.

537–9   The flag was decorated (*emblazed*) like a Roman standard with jewels, shining gold thread, coats of arms, and battle souvenirs. What does the comparison to a meteor suggest to you (see note to I 594–9 for one suggestion)?

540   **Sonorous metal**   the resonant instruments mentioned in 532 above.

541   **the universal host upsent**   the whole army sent up (the last word is turned round to fit the metre).

542   **tore Hell's concave**   penetrated the arched roof (see I 298).

543   **reign of Chaos**   the kingdom outside Hell, ruled by Chaos and his consort, Night (we visit them II 959–63).

546   **orient**   lustrous, bright.

547   **helms**   helmets.

548   **serried**   close-packed.

549   **depth immeasurable**   impossible to measure the width of the column. (One of several places where Milton suggests that the fallen angels are numberless).

550   **In perfect phalanx ... mood**   in exact formation to appropriate modal music. The Dorian mode (*mood*), which is the white-note scale beginning on D, was associated in ancient Greece with military music.

551–9   Milton, an ardent musician, here describes the effect of music, as he does again II 546–54; in both cases emotions are controlled and soothed (*swage*) rather than aroused. The Dorian music here also seems able to control virtue, by transforming the emotion of rage into a steely composure (*noblest temper*) and willed courage (*deliberate valour*). Aristotle said that this mode induced a *settled temper* and Plato said it gave courage. (Prince ed. of *P.L.*)

556–7   **Nor wanting ... thoughts**   not lacking power to lessen and soothe *troubled thoughts* by brief serious phrases (*touches*).

558   Note the soothing effect of the repeated *and*.

560–1   **Breathing united force ... in silence**   Compare Homer's *Iliad* 3:8: *The Greeks marched in silence, breathing courage.*

561   **charmed**   Are the angels being deluded by the music?

563   **horrid front**   the front line bristling with spears (see note to I 51).

568   **traverse**   across.

570   **visages and stature**   faces and size.

571   **number**   See note to 549 above.

572   **Distends ... and hardening**   enlarges, puffs up, and then hardens (compare *Daniel* 5:20 where God deposes King Nebbuchadnezzar because *his heart was lifted up, and his mind hardened in pride*). But do you altogether despise Satan here?

573–6   **for never ... cranes**   For never since the creation of Man could a concentrated (*embodied*) human force be assembled which, when compared to these, would be worth more than the Pygmy army. Pygmies are a race of very small people in Africa; who (according to *Iliad* III 1–5) were frequently attacked and defeated by flocks of cranes (birds); they are referred to again I 780.

575   **infantry**   foot-soldiers (with a pun on infant, suggesting smallness).

576   **though**   even if; introduces a comparison of Satan's army with the lesser ones of the Greek, Arthurian, and French legends.

576–8   **Giant brood ... Ilium**   even if the Titans (already mentioned 198 and 510) who fought the Olympian gods at Phlegra were joined with the gods and Greek heroes who fought at Thebes and Troy (*Ilium*).

579   **auxiliar**   helping (according to Homer, the Greek gods were involved in these human wars).

579   **resounds**   is famous.

579–81   **romance of Uther's son**   stories (known collectively as *romances*) of King Arthur, son of Uther Pendragon, and his surrounding (*begirt*) Round Table of knights from Britain and Brittany (*Armorica*).

581   **begirt**   surrounded.

582–7   Milton finally refers to the legendary armies of the ninth-century Emperor Charlemagne (*Charlemain*), who defended France from Muslim (*infidel*) and African invaders till he and his 12 chief knights (*peerage*) were defeated at Roncesvalles (not *Fontarabbia*). The hypnotic place-names are mostly from Italian epics like *Orlando Furioso*.

583   **Jousted**   fought on horseback with lances.

585   **Biserta**   the port from which the African king Agramante embarked.

Third Description of Satan: He Weeps for his Army: Lines 587–621

Here we are told of the physical and moral degeneration of Satan, but we may feel how much remains (including what remains of his virtue) rather than how much is lost. The comparisons of Satan with a tower and the obscured sun suggest he is god-like, as these are similes for God in the Bible (for example, *II Samuel* 32; *Psalms* 84:11), but also note words which suggest he is damaged and dangerous (for example, *ruined*). He seems very human here, and we are allowed to share in his feelings, although he seems determined to conceal them even from himself. Look at words like *followers* and *faithful*, used of the army. Does Satan's *remorse* make his continuing the war more or less forgivable?

587–8   **Thus far ... yet observed**   although these were so far above comparison, yet Satan could see them all.

594–9   **as when ... monarchs**   Epic similes comparing Satan to the sun obscured by mist or the shadow of the moon. Since God is more naturally associated with the sun, and Satan with the moon, what does the *misty air* and *dim eclipse* which change the sun's light here suggest about Satan?

595   **horizontal**   a transferred epithet as it is the beam, not the air, which is horizontal. Note the assonance with *Shorn* in 596.

597–9   **disastrous twilight ... monarchs**   Eclipses, like comets, were supposed to predict natural disasters and political unrest, particularly as one accompanied Christ's death (*Luke* 23:44); in what ways will Satan have this effect?

601 **thunder** the weapon which cast him out of Heaven (see note to I 93).

601 **entrenched** furrowed.

603 **dauntless** fearless.

603 **considerate** deliberate (from *considerare* (Latin), meaning to think).

606 **fellows ... followers** one letter shifts the meaning from companion to victim.

607 Compare with I 84.

609–10 **amerced/Of Heaven** fined or deprived of Heaven.

612–15 Epic simile comparing the army to a lightning-struck forest left standing on burnt soil (*blasted heath*); compare I 292–6 above. What does the phrase *stately growth* (referring to branches) tell you about the angels?

616–18 The main body of the army forms a close semi-circle around Satan and the other leaders (*peers*).

619 **essayed** tried (to speak).

619 **scorn** his own pride. Do you admire his tears or his suppression of them more?

621 **interwove** interwoven, mixed.

Satan Gives his Army an Account of the Past and a Plan for the Future: Lines 622–69

This is Satan's first political speech and its purpose is to influence rather than inform his army, though he does tell them for the first time about Earth. What does he want them to feel, or not to feel? How does he characterize God? Do you think the complexity of the sentences suggests that Satan is hiding something?

We can divide the speech into the following sections:

• the flattering address or **exordium** (622–3)

• the first argument or **narratio** (626–30) which attempts to explain the past, and is supported by three **confirmationes** or supporting arguments (631–4, 635–7, 637–42)

• the second narratio (643–56), which looks to the future, and is supported by one confirmatio (657–9)

• the **conclusio** summoning a council (659–62) and giving the motion for debate (what kind of war to pursue).

622　**myriads**　vast numbers.

624　**not inglorious ... dire**　the battle was glorious even if the outcome was terrible.

625　**testifies**　witnesses, proves.

626–31　Satan's first argument (the narratio and confirmatio of 626–42) is that no-one, however prophetic or knowledgeable, could have *feared* (main verb) failure. Note how the rhetorical questions and the repeated auxiliaries (*could ... could ... can*) communicate his incredulity.

627　**presaging**　predicting.

630　**repulse**　check.

631–4　**For who ... shall fail to reascend?**　For no-one could believe they will fail to re-ascend, even though they are now (*yet*) experiencing loss. The argument that the angels, being made of fire, the lightest element, will re-ascend, is used again at II 75–6.

632　**puissant legions**　powerful divisions.

633　**emptied Heaven**　In fact (V 710) only a third of the angels were cast out.

634　**native seat**　original homeland (implying they have a right to be there).

635–7　**be witness ... our hopes**　I call all angels to vouch for the truth that it was not because I took the wrong advice, or tried to avoid dangers, that we lost. Does this absolve him of responsibility for the failure?

639–40　**old repute,/Consent or custom**　Three reasons for retaining the monarchy: its fame, its acceptance by the people, and its long history. Sneering at these means Satan has to find other reasons for justifying his own rule at II 18–21.

640　**regal state**　royal grandeur (as opposed to practical *strength*, 641).

642　**tempted our attempt**　The pun reinforces the lie that God enticed them to attack him by appearing weak.

642　**wrought**　made, brought about.

643–56   Satan's second narratio. God creates the Universe after the fall of the angels, but Satan says he has heard a rumour of the plan, though he prefers to see *space* as the creative force; we hear more about his plan at II 380.

644–5   **So as not … provoked**   we will neither provoke nor respond if God provokes us (again note the characterization of God).

646–7   **to work … effected not**   to plan secretly (*close design*) how *fraud or guile* may achieve what force failed to achieve.

648   **who overcomes … foe**   the whole phrase is the object of *find*.

650   **rife**   prevalent.

651   **ere long**   before long (see note to 643–56).

653–4   Both here and at the next mention of Man (II 345–51) we feel Satan inflaming the jealousy of the other angels (*sons of Heaven*).

656   **eruption**   ascent (but it sounds distorted and violent).

660   **Peace is despaired**   We have abandoned hope of peace (though this is not true of the angels: see II 227, 292).

662   **understood**   one of a number of words in the speech to suggest a policy of a secret, deceitful hostility.

663   **out-flew**   flew out (like *upsent* 541 above).

666   **illumined**   lit up.

666–7   **highly … Highest**   What is the effect of the pun?

668   **Clashed**   A traditional Roman 'hurrah' was to clash swords on shields.

The Building of Pandæmonium: Lines 670–751

Pandæmonium is Milton's invented name for the infernal Parliament building. It is built on the model of a Greek temple, appropriate for the Classical soldiers which the angels are impersonating at the moment. It also has the ornateness which Milton may have seen in Italy in Classical-style Catholic churches such as St. Peter's cathedral in Rome. Its aesthetic values are those of Heaven, but its imagery is that of a rather gross human body (*scurf, belched, womb* etc). Is it a noble attempt to make *a Heaven of Hell* (I 255) or merely an imitation, a theatrical, temporary, empty illusion?

670   **grisly**   horrifying.

674   **The work of sulphur**   Sulphur (characterized by a flaky *scurf*) was supposed to be the agent which produced the other metals.

675–8   Epic simile comparing the angels to foot-soldiers (*pioneers*) preparing a battlefield; what is the effect of the comparison?

677   **Forerun**   go before an army to make preparations.

678   **cast**   throw up.

678   **Mammon**   the Biblical personification of wealth and worldly values; see *Matthew* 6:24, *Luke* 16:13.

679   **least erected**   most ignoble (he speaks last at the Council).

681   **downward bent**   Directions are crucial in Milton for love, virtue, and creativity should always be directed towards God and not away from him or into the self.

682   **Heaven's pavement**   In *Revelation* 21: 21 we are told that *the street of the [Heavenly] city was pure gold, as it were transparent glass.*

683–4   **aught divine ... vision beatific**   than anything else which the angelic and mystical (*beatific*) vision was able to enjoy.

685   **men also**   The Classical author Ovid saw the mining of wealth from Mother Earth as part of the fall of Man from the original Golden Age (*Metamorphosis* I 137–42), and Spenser has Mammon mining gold in Hell in *Fairie Queene* II vii (1596).

686   **impious**   irreligious, disrespectful.

686–90   **bowels, wound, ribs, ransacked the centre**   more body imagery.

690   **admire**   wonder at.

692   **precious bane**   valuable poison.

694   **Babel**   The tower of Babel aimed to 'reach unto Heaven' (*Genesis* 11:4–9).

694   **Memphian kings**   The Egyptian kings or pharaohs built the enormous pyramids near Cairo (*Memphis*); compare II 483–5.

697   **reprobate**   rejected, proved bad.

697   Note here and at 711 the speed with which the edifice is built; what does this suggest to you?

700   **Nigh**   nearby.

700   **cells**   workshops (with underfloor furnaces).

702   **Sluiced** channelled.

703   **Founded** (*found out* in *P.L.* ed. II, 1671) melted (main verb) as in a foundry.

704   **Severing each kind and scummed the bullion dross** by their *art* or skill they separate the ores and skim the impurities (*dross*) from the pure metals (*bullion*). Or maybe *bullion dross* is another oxymoron?

705   **A third** a third group (the first mined, the second smelted).

706–7   **A various mould ... hollow nook** a complex mould (representing the shape of the whole building carved in reverse into the ground) into whose detailed indentations the molten metal is conveyed, by a clever system, forming a hollow shape.

708–11   Just as one expulsion of wind (*blast, exhalation*) can fill many organ pipes, so a musical breath filled the mould from underneath and blew the hollow building inside-out on top of the ground (like a plastic toy). What is suggested to you by this pneumatic building-method and sound effects (712)?

710   **Anon** at once.

711   **exhalation** outburst of air or wind (suggesting what?).

712   **dulcet symphonies** sweet instrumental music. Musical proportions were supposedly allied to architectural ones, so Thebes and Troy were also constructed to the sound of music.

713–14   **pilasters round/Were** set squared columns were arranged around (probably against the wall).

714–16   **Doric pillars ... graven** an inner colonnade of pillars with Doric capitals (same connotations as the music at I 550) supported the golden beam (*architrave*) leading up to a projecting *cornice*, on which was carved in high relief (*bossy sculptures*) the decorative *frieze*. The architrave could go across the front or around the whole space. The effect is Classically impressive but clearly pagan.

717   **fretted** carved in decorative patterns usually of intersecting lines, but Hamlet admired the heavens *fretted with golden fire* (II 2.313). Though the angels themselves have never seen the sky, we recognize their roof is an imitation.

717–18   **Babylon, Alcairo** Monumental capital cities of the oppressive kingdoms of Assyria and Egypt; Babylon was in particular the focus of evil in the Bible (*Revelation* 17:5) and became an insulting name for Rome, home of the Pope. See the gigantic Assyrian sculptures in the British Museum.

720   **Belus, Serapis**   the Assyrian form of Baal, and the Egyptian Osiris; see note to 419–56 and 478 above.

723   **Th'ascending pile/stood fixed**   the edifice stopped rising at its proper height. In 1637 a court masque (musical entertainment) included a scene where 'the earth open'd, and there rose up a richly-adorned pallace ... with proticos vaulted, on pillasters of rich rustick work; their bases and capitels of gold. Above these ran an architrave, freese, and coronis of the same.' (quoted from M. Hughes ed. of *P.L*). In what ways is Pandæmonium like a piece of scenery?

724   **brazen folds**   brass leaves.

724   **discover** reveal.

727   **subtle magic**   clever contrivance (as opposed to God's ability to hang the stars in the sky).

728–9   **lamps ... naphtha and asphaltus**   lamps containing oil from bituminous rock (*naphtha*) and hanging baskets (*cressets*) holding lumps of burning asphalt; the ingredients of Hell used to imitate the Heavenly city which *had no need of the sun, nor of the moon ... for the glory of God did light it.* (*Revelation* 23:23).

734   **sceptreed angels**   high-ranking angels who lived in towers.

736   **Exalted**   glorified.

737   **hierarchy**   his place in the hierarchy of *orders,* as in an army. How do you respond to this glimpse of heavenly society? Does it suggest the monarchy and perhaps nobility which Milton himself had sought to overthrow. Or does it symbolize creation's ordered ascent to God?

739–40   **in Ausonian land ... Mulciber**   in Italy (*Ausonia*) men called the Greek god Hephaestus *Mulciber* (or Vulcan). As smith and artist he built the palaces of the gods on Mount Olympus before he was thrown down by Zeus (*Iliad* I 588–95).

746   **Lemnos th'Ægæan isle**   *Lemnos* in the Ægæan sea, where Mulciber landed.

747   **Erring**   Milton claims that the story of the fall of Mulciber

is a misrepresentation of the true story of the fall of the angels (I 50–1 above and *Isaiah* 14:12–15). Why does Milton make Mulciber sound so beautiful, and why does he emphasize this word by its position?

748   **nor aught availed**   nor did it help him.

750   **engines**   contrivances (such as the *subtle magic* of 727).

The Fallen Angels Take Possession of Pandæmonium: Lines 752–98

Having done so much to magnify and glorify the angels, Milton seems here to be using mock-epic techniques to diminish them in our eyes. A mock-epic laughs at the form and the heroic qualities of the epic; Pope's *Rape of the Lock*, which is a parody of *Paradise Lost*, is an example. The passage is almost a comic interlude before the solemn business of Book II. What do the comparisons with insects (compare I 595), Pygmies, and elves suggest to you? Why does Milton have them change both their costume and their size?

753   **sovereign power**   Satan's royal power.

753   **awful**   awe-inspiring.

756   **Pandæmonium**   'All the Demons.' (Milton's coinage from Greek words, which has come to mean a chaotic assembly).

758   **squared**   drawn up in a square.

759   **By place or choice the worthiest**   representatives to attend the Parliament are chosen by rank or election. Should we compare this democracy to the rigid hierarchy of Heaven (see I 737)?

763–6   Milton compares the hall to a huge crowded tent where Saracen knights were challenged (*defied*) before their sultan's (*soldan's*) throne. Saracens were the Muslim (*paynim*) opponents of the Christians in the Crusades; this continues the Romance comparisons of 579–87 above; the angels seem to have now changed their costume from that of the Classical army.

766   **career with lance** jousting, or horseback fighting with lances.

768   Note the onomatopoeic alliteration.

768–75   Epic simile comparing the angels to bees active in spring-time (when the sun enters *Taurus* in April). Some swarm *in clusters*, others collect nectar from flowers; others walk about and discuss (*expatiate and confer*) on the plank that goes into the hive, which is rubbed with attractive oils (*balm*). Of course they only imagine they have control over *their state affairs*. How many more points of comparison can you find between the simile and the angels, and what is its effect on your attitude to them?

773   **straw-built citadel**   castle built of straw (compare the *Three Little Pigs*).

776   **straitened**   confined into too narrow a space.

777–80   The innumerable angels shrink themselves from the size of giants to tiny elves.

781   **Indian mount**   the Himalayas, beyond which the Classical historian Pliny erroneously located the pygmies, who really live in central Africa.

781–8   Epic simile comparing the diminished angels with elves. Note the care with which Milton sets the scene at night (as at I 207), when the moon provokes and witnesses (*sits arbitress*) magic and madness, and the fairies play sinister yet compelling music. How does the comparison warn us about the angels?

793–5   The chief angels (*seraphic lords*) have not diminished themselves, but sit in special seats in private council (*secret conclave*). What does this tell you about Satan's style of government?

797   **Frequent and full**   crowded and without absentees.

798   **consult**   consultation.